MAKING SENSE OF THE BIBLE

MAKING SENSE
of the
BIBLE

Literary Type
as an Approach to Understanding

MARSHALL D. JOHNSON

WILLIAM B. EERDMANS PUBLISHING COMPANY
GRAND RAPIDS, MICHIGAN / CAMBRIDGE, U.K.

Wm. B. Eerdmans Publishing Co.
255 Jefferson Ave. S.E., Grand Rapids, Michigan 49503 /
P.O. Box 163, Cambridge CB3 9PU U.K.

Printed in the United States of America

06 05 04 03 02   7 6 5 4 3 2 1

Library of Congress Cataloging-in-Publication Data

Johnson, Marshall D.
Making sense of the Bible: literary type as an approach to understanding /
Marshall D. Johnson.
p.   cm.
Includes bibliographical references and index.
ISBN 0-8028-4919-9 (pbk.: alk. paper)
1. Bible as literature.   I. Title.

BS535.J64 2002
809'.93522 — dc21
2001053865

www.eerdmans.com

In memory of
W. D. Davies

Contents

Acknowledgments   ix

1. Introduction: What Are You Reading?   1

2. Morals, Manners, and the Good Life: Wisdom Literature   9

3. Praise, Lament, and Thanksgiving: Poetry of Worship   26

4. The Appeal to the Past: Historical
   and Quasi-Historical Narratives   34

5. Justice, Judgment, and the Fate of Nations:
   Prophetic Literature   54

6. Regulating Life: Legal Collections   66

7. The Appeal to the Future: Apocalyptic Literature   73

8. I Want You to Know: Letters   80

9. Redemptive Persuasion: The Gospels   92

10. Conclusion: Making Sense of the Bible   141

Appendix A: Forms of Ancient Hebrew Poetry   144

CONTENTS

Appendix B: Major Literary Types and Selected
Biblical References   149

Suggestions for Further Reading   151

Maps   156

Index   160

Acknowledgments

I am grateful to all who have made this book possible, especially those who guided me into the rarified world of biblical studies and whose insights are often reflected in the following chapters. Chief among these is W. D. Davies (1912–2001) of blessed memory, revered teacher and friend over several decades. Important also are the professional publishing colleagues and friends of the past several years who made me more aware of the realities of an intriguing and competitive world. Special thanks go to my past and present colleagues of the Fortress Press team, whose academic publishing program I continue to hold in high regard. In addition, I thank those whose comments on parts of this book have impelled me to take a second and third look at some vexing issues. For the formulation of perspectives, structure, and details, however, I freely accept responsibility.

For their courtesy, encouragement, and professionalism, I am indebted to Jon Pott, vice president and editor-in-chief at Eerdmans, and his able colleagues in the editorial, production, publicity, and sales areas of this venerable publishing company.

One person in particular encouraged me to begin and to complete this project, discussed various issues of structure and content, and read the entire work with a critical eye for clarity and effectiveness. Special thanks to my wife, Alice Joy.

I

Introduction: What Are You Reading?

No book in the Western world has evoked more diverse responses than the perennial bestseller, the Bible. It is appealed to as a prime authority by evangelists, nominal Christians, militias, politicians, and social reformers — not to mention the large number of organized Christian denominations and branches of Judaism — and we wonder at the variety of interpretations given it and the conflicting claims made on its behalf. How is it possible that biblical authority can be cited for widely divergent causes? In light of such postmodern confusion, can ordinary persons make sense of this body of ancient literature?

A Matter of Distance and Difference

A good part of the difficulty in making sense of the Bible is the gap of 2000 years between the writing of the Bible and our time. There are enormous differences between the ancient Semitic and Hellenistic societies that produced the Bible and the postmodern Western, technologically-based communities of the present. Essential to understanding the Bible is an appreciation of the cultural distance between these two worlds. Language, literacy, geography, economic realities, myths, children's stories, tribalism, traditional values — all these and much more shape a people's culture. At the same time, I believe that it is not necessary for contemporary persons to become experts in the social history of antiquity to appreciate much of what the ancient writers were about.

Biblical writers often deal with matters about which the first readers were well informed and we are not. This is obviously the case with respect to letters, but it applies also to other literature, for example, prophetic oracles. In cases where the original context of a document is presupposed or only partly alluded to, we are forced to read carefully, sometimes between the lines.

We might also be hindered from making sense of the Bible by our own preconceptions about what the Bible says — or what we think it should say. Christians, for example, often read Old Testament passages through New Testament eyes. Reading any document freshly, with the intent of discovering at least something of the thought-world and mind of the writer, requires curiosity, concentration, and a certain willingness to allow our prior thoughts to be challenged. How can we approach the Bible in a way that does justice both to the integrity of our concerns and interests and also to the integrity of the writers' intentions and purposes?

A new awareness of the subjective aspects of reading ancient texts — not least biblical texts — emerged in the latter half of the 20th century. At the same time, the growing involvement of women and persons from minority backgrounds in technical biblical studies led to the reshaping of questions that readers brought to the texts. This often provided dramatic evidence not only of the patriarchal bias of ancient texts but also of the provincialism of much of traditional European-male biblical scholarship — without denying the impressive results achieved in former generations. These new influences brought refreshment to the established discipline of biblical studies but also an awareness of the subjectivity that is necessarily involved in all attempts to interpret texts.

Some postmodern theoreticians today argue that, because interpretation always and necessarily takes place in the mind of the reader, no one interpretation can claim to be "correct" or superior to another. While granting the tentative nature of interpreting ancient texts, I remain convinced of one basic principle, which underlies this book: *all writings must have had a meaning for their first readers* — or, at least, the author must have thought so. This principle applies throughout the following chapters, but it perhaps affects most acutely those who read from a Christian context. How could a psalm or a prophetic text written several centuries before the time of Jesus refer specifically to him (for one example, see the discussion of Isaiah 7 in Chapter 5, below)? The challenge of uncovering what might have been the "author's intention," however, is often daunting. How can we responsibly approach an ancient text with the hope of understanding? I propose one way to begin.

Recognizing that there are diverse kinds of literature within the Bible, each with distinctive perspectives, can be an effective first step in making sense of what many readers have found to be confusing, arcane, or contradictory in the Bible. This approach also can go far to explain the variety of effects the Bible has had in history. By identifying the characteristics, intentions, concerns, and thought-complexes of each literary form, it is possible to hear the biblical writers afresh and possible also for us to respond to their concerns in an appropriate way. Each of the eight major literary types described in the following chapters has its own subtypes — in some cases, a good number of them. Liturgical materials include hymns, laments, enthronement psalms, and others (and these also have distinctive subgroups). This book, however, focuses on the basic literary forms as a first step toward understanding.

Whatever else we may believe about the Bible, no one can deny that it is a collection of literature. Generally speaking, the Bible comes to us in the recognizable and well-documented literary forms of the ancient world — letters, laws, records, liturgies, quasi-historical reports, love poems, prophetic oracles, and more. Much of this ancient extrabiblical material was "high literature," that is, intended for publication, but there have also been discovered masses of documents written for everyday needs on simple materials like papyrus. Fortunately for us, recognizing a specific literary genre does not generally require a good knowledge of other languages or even a detailed knowledge of ancient societies, necessary as these are for scholarly research. The larger literary forms can often be recognized by reading a translation of the Bible.

The major literary forms in the Bible to be described in the following chapters are wisdom literature, liturgical materials, quasi-historical material, prophetic writings, collections of laws and precepts, apocalyptic literature, letters, and Gospels. I describe the central features of each, including both formal aspects and emphases of content that can give readers a sense of what to expect from each specific literary form and how to approach it. The compilers of wisdom literature had quite different interests compared with the prophets, for example, and both differed considerably from the compilers of laws or liturgical materials or the relating of events from the past. A sense of these differences gives the reader a head start on the path to understanding the text and avoiding pitfalls.

In a book of this scope, a *selection* of examples of each literary type must be made. In spite of this limitation, I believe that the texts discussed in the following chapters serve to illustrate the broad features of each form. Where appropriate, materials from both Testaments are included in the discussion of each type.

The Literature in General

Our Bible has its origins as the sacred Scripture of two religious traditions, the Old Testament from the ancient Israelites and Jews and the New Testament from the Christians. The terms "Old Testament" and "New Testament" are coinages of the Christians. The term "Hebrew Bible" designates the Scripture of Judaism and the language in which almost all of the Old Testament material was written (half of the book of Daniel and parts of Ezra are written in Aramaic, a language related to Hebrew).

THE OLD TESTAMENT

The order of books in the Old Testament of English Bibles is not that of the Hebrew Bible, which has three parts:

1. The *Torah* ("instruction" or "law") consists of the books of Genesis, Exodus, Leviticus, Numbers, and Deuteronomy — the same order

as in the English Bibles. The term "Pentateuch" is also used to designate these five books.

2. The *Nevi'im* ("prophets") consist of (a) the "former prophets," the four books Joshua, Judges, Samuel (counted as one book), Kings (counted as one), and (b) the "latter prophets," Isaiah, Jeremiah, Ezekiel, and the "scroll of the Twelve" (the so-called minor prophets). In antiquity each of the four books of the "latter prophets" occupied one scroll of approximately the same length.

3. The *Kethuvim* ("writings") include the remainder of the books found in the Old Testament, including the Psalms, Proverbs, Job, Daniel, Chronicles, and others.

The Old Testament is also known by the acronym *Tanakh,* a word formed by the initial consonants of the words Torah, Nevi'im, and Kethuvim.

The threefold division of the Hebrew Bible reflects the approximate time at which these sections came to be considered authoritative by the Jewish community. The term "canon" is used to refer to books accepted as authoritative — as "Scripture" — by a religious community. For Jewish communities, the Torah is the core. It was the earliest section to have been canonized — at some point soon after the end of the Babylonian exile, possibly with the arrival of Ezra in Jerusalem around 428 B.C.E.*
The Prophets were gathered as a literary collection approximately 200 B.C.E., and the final decisions on the canon of the Hebrew Bible emerged toward the end of the 1st century C.E., in the decades following the restructuring of Judaism after the fall of Jerusalem to the Romans in 70 C.E.

The order of books in the Old Testament (in the English Bible) reflects the sequence of material in the ancient Greek translation.

The diverse literature of the Old Testament originated during a period of nearly 1000 years and was written by priests, prophets, annalists, sages, apocalypticists, and others. Nonetheless, as the centuries passed,

---

*The scholarly convention of using B.C.E., "before the common era," and C.E., "common era," to designate B.C. and A.D., respectively, is followed in this book.

several common emphases emerged with clarity in almost all the literary types: the oneness of God, membership in God's covenant with Moses and the people, adherence to the law (Torah) of God, the one people of God, the centrality of the temple in Jerusalem, and a variety of hopes for the future of the people in their own land.

An interesting linguistic and religious problem is the rendition in English of the various Hebrew terms for God, especially the personal name indicated by the consonants YHWH (the Hebrew language has no letters for vowels). This name of God has been and is considered so holy by religious Jews from late antiquity until today that it cannot be pronounced. English translations of the Bible usually render this term "LORD" (initial capital followed by small caps), reflecting the Jewish tradition of reading the Hebrew word *Adonai* (Lord) where these four letters occur in the text. In this book I indicate the occurrence of this term alternately by "YHWH," "LORD," or "Yahweh" (the presumed pronunciation of the term in antiquity).

Numerous Jewish writings were excluded from the Hebrew Bible. Among the more important of these "deuterocanonical" ("second canon") writings are the Apocrypha, Jewish books considered Scripture by the Roman Catholic church, the Greek church, and other churches because of tradition and also because they were included in most copies of the ancient Greek and Latin translations of the Old Testament. Most books in the Apocrypha were written between 200 B.C.E. and 150 C.E. Some of these books have high intrinsic value, especially Sirach (Ecclesiasticus), Wisdom, and 1 Maccabees.

THE NEW TESTAMENT

The New Testament contains 27 documents, all written originally in the everyday Greek of the Mediterranean world of the 1st century C.E. Thirteen of these are letters attributed to the apostle Paul (some of which are the oldest Christian documents extant); eight are general letters of unknown authorship; one is a narrative account of the origin of the Christian church; one is an apocalypse; and four are Gospels — a unique genre in several respects. In Christian churches these books, along with the books of the Hebrew Bible (and, for some churches, the Apocrypha), are considered Scripture — authoritative for the doctrines and life of their members. There is a chronological overlap between the writing of the latest New Testament books (perhaps 1-2 Timothy; Titus; 2 Peter; and the Gospel of John) and other early Christian literature, like the moral manual Didache, 1 Clement (written around 95 C.E.), and the letters of Ignatius (martyred in Rome in approximately 117 C.E.). Several scholars have argued that the Gospel of Thomas antedates some of the Gospels in the New Testament, although others date it to the 2nd century.

The variety of writing styles, theology, values, and presupposed social location of the New Testament writers is broad indeed. Paul and the author of 1 Peter, for example, advise their readers to subject themselves to the political powers of the time, but the book of Revelation looks forward to the cataclysmic destruction of all worldly powers in a series of acts of divine wrath. Some writers emphasize what Jesus *taught,* and others his *death* in Jerusalem. Is there a common experience or set of beliefs behind this diversity? All parts of the New Testament presuppose an ultimate significance for Jesus. These early Christian writers granted authority to what they remembered Jesus to have said, and they preserved traditions about his death. Most importantly, they believed that God had resurrected Jesus after his death and taken him into the divine presence, and they struggled to understand and explain this. The birth of the Christian church coincides with the emergence of the resurrection faith.

With the exception of some of Paul's letters, it is truly amazing how little we know about the origin of these documents — date of writing, authorship, place of writing, and intended readers. All four Gospels, Acts, and the letter to the Hebrews are anonymous (the name of the author is not given in the content of the document), and some of the remaining books may have been issued under a pseudonym.

Paul's letters (written 45-65 C.E.) and possibly two or more other books in the New Testament (James, Jude, and others) antedate the writing of the Gospels (65-95 C.E.). Although Jesus stands at the begin-

ning of Christianity, and traditions about his words and deeds circulated from the earliest period — probably even before his death — the
Gospels will be the last literary form considered in this book.

2

Morals, Manners, and the Good Life: Wisdom Literature

Because "wisdom literature" (proverbs and reflection on the meaning of life) is found in all human societies and in all ages of history, it is among the most familiar and accessible material in the Bible and is therefore taken up here in first place. Consider the timeless appeal of the following:

Pride goes before destruction,
    and a haughty spirit before a fall.   (Prov. 16:18)

The human spirit will endure sickness;
    but a broken spirit — who can bear?   (Prov. 18:14)

A word fitly spoken
    is like apples of gold in a setting of silver.   (Prov. 25:11)

A good name is better than precious ointment,
    and the day of death, than the day of birth.   (Eccl. 7:1)

My days are swifter than a weaver's shuttle,
    and come to their end without hope.   (Job 7:6)

Do not judge, so that you may not be judged.   (Matt. 7:1)

9

In everything do to others as you would have them do to you.

(Matt. 7:12)

Proverbs, riddles, and other "wisdom sayings" are among the oldest fragments in our Bible. Jeremiah and Ezekiel quote and refute an old proverb that suggests inherited guilt:

The parents have eaten sour grapes,
    and the children's teeth are set on edge.

(Jer. 31:29 = Ezek. 18:2)

Other ancient sayings are found in 1 Sam. 10:12; 24:13; Jer. 23:38; Ezek. 16:44; and 1 Kgs. 20:11.

The Nature and Origin of Old Testament Wisdom Literature

Wisdom literature is the primary genre of the books of Proverbs, Job, Ecclesiastes, and several of the Psalms (for example, Pss. 1, 37, 49, 73, 127). In the Apocrypha the books of Ben Sira (Sirach or Ecclesiasticus) and Wisdom (Wisdom of Solomon) also fall into this category, as does the "letter" of James in the New Testament.

The Hebrew word *hokmah*, usually translated "wisdom," is broader in meaning than that English word. At least in early Israelite times (see Judg. 5:29; 2 Sam. 13:3 ["crafty"]; 14:2, 20; 20:16; Isa. 10:13; 29:14; Jer. 8:8-9; 9:23; 18:18), it suggested practical skill and technical expertise such as could be learned through life experience — the kind of professional savvy that leads to success in life. As such, the term is applied in the Old Testament to artists, musicians, craftspersons, weavers, goldsmiths, sailors, lamenters, temple singers, and soldiers who are skilled in their work. When applied to a proverb or discourse or piece of literature, the term came to denote both (1) advice on practical matters — manners and morals — such as in the books of Proverbs and Ben Sira and (2) reflections on larger questions of meaning — or the absence of meaning — in life, such as in the books of Job, Ecclesiastes, and the Wisdom of Solomon. Moreover, in what appear to be the earlier traditions of such material (for example, parts of Prov. 10–22 and 25–29 as well as passages listed above), Old Testament wisdom traditions in the beginning show few signs of what we would call religious piety. They concentrated instead on practical matters of personal life. As the centuries passed, however, wisdom literature became increasingly connected with the basic features of Israel's relation to God, so that it could be said, "The fear of the LORD [Yahweh] is the beginning of knowledge [or wisdom]" (Prov. 1:7).

In the passage of time, King Solomon (ruled 961-922 B.C.E.) came to be celebrated as the great Israelite patron of wisdom literature. This sentiment is echoed in 1 Kgs. 4:29-34:

> God gave Solomon very great wisdom, discernment, and breadth of understanding as vast as the sand on the seashore, so that Solomon's wisdom surpassed the wisdom of all the people of the east, and all the wisdom of Egypt. He was wiser than anyone else, wiser than Ethan the Ezrahite, and Heman, Calcol, and Darda, children of Mahol; his fame spread throughout all the surrounding nations. He composed three thousand proverbs, and his songs numbered a thousand and five. He would speak of trees, from the cedar that is in Lebanon to the hyssop that grows in the wall; he would speak of animals, and birds, and reptiles, and fish. People came from all the nations to hear the wisdom of Solomon; they came from all the kings of the earth who had heard of his wisdom.

This passage makes several assertions about the nature and origin of Hebrew wisdom literature:

1. Israel's wisdom was of the same barrel as that of "the people of the east" (Sumer, Babylon, Assyria) and "the wisdom of Egypt." Indeed, there are abundant examples of such extrabiblical wisdom, much of it considerably older than that of the Old Testament. The Old Testament itself asserts that this kind of literature is not unique to the

Bible. It is probable that some Egyptian wisdom traditions — the oldest in the ancient Near East — came to Israel by way of their southern neighbor, Edom (see Jer. 49:7 and Obad. 8).

2. The content of early Hebrew wisdom involved practical, everyday concerns and included references to common plants and animals.

3. There was a class or profession of sages or scribes. Jer. 18:18 lists three professional classes: the *priest* gives instruction, presumably in the laws; the *prophet* conveys the word (oracles of God); and the *sage* gives counsel. Through what agency the sage conducted his professional activity and earned his living, the sources, unfortunately, do not say. Did the royal court have an academy for young males from landed families to supply the need of the state bureaucracy for documents? Were sages employed by wealthy families? To judge by the lack of interest in communal worship in the wisdom literature generally, sages were not closely connected to the temple in Jerusalem.

4. Although 1 Kings engages in a bit of hyperbole with respect to Solomon's 3000 proverbs and 1005 songs, Solomon came to be remembered as the great patriarch of Israelite wisdom literature. Tradition assigns to him the authorship of much of the book of Proverbs, Ecclesiastes, the Song of Solomon, the Wisdom of Solomon, and later books, like the Psalms of Solomon and the Odes of Solomon.

The contents of the books of Proverbs, Job, and Ecclesiastes generally suggest that the sages instructed young men from prominent families. (1) The first 10 sections of the book of Proverbs begin with the words "my child" (or "my son," RSV). Warnings against sexual immorality, however, show that the instruction was for postpubescent males. (2) Moreover, the content suggests that young men — not women — are in mind. Women are mentioned, but mostly as mothers, wives, or harlots. (3) The young men are from prominent families: the bad habits to be avoided were sometimes expensive, and the virtues inculcated were often possible only for the well off (for example, table manners at banquets). Especially indicative is one of the main themes of Proverbs: success comes to those who deserve it by diligence, hard work, and, in some texts, piety.

Striking Distinctive Features

Israelite wisdom literature offers striking contrasts with other literary forms in the Old Testament:

- Until the time of the writing of Ben Sira and Wisdom of Solomon, references to Israel's history — past, present, or future — are generally absent in wisdom literature. The two heroic epochs — of Moses and of David — are not alluded to. Nor is there mention of future judgment or restoration, as the prophets so typically emphasize.

- The life of the individual — not society or the nation — is the focus of wisdom literature, whether it deals with manners and morals or with reflection on the meaning of existence. This concentration on personal life partly explains the seeming disinterest in Israel's history.

- Only occasionally is there reference, either positive or negative, to the forms of Israel's worship (sacrifices, rituals, priesthood, festivals). The work of the sage does not significantly overlap with that of the priest.

- The distinctive medium of Israelite prophecy — oracles of the LORD, in which the first-person pronoun refers to Yahweh — is missing. Instead of direct revelation, the sage offers advice derived from reflection on human experience, and this is often articulated by Lady Wisdom — wisdom personified.

- If the prophets often speak on behalf of the disenfranchised, wisdom literature reflects the thinking and values of the established classes of society — the landed nobility and royalty.

- To a degree greater than most other literary forms in the Bible, wisdom literature is an international form, practiced by the early Israelites in much the same way as it was carried out in Babylon and Egypt.

The Book of Proverbs

The book of Proverbs is a collection of collections, as we learn from the seven headings within the book:

- The proverbs of Solomon son of David, king of Israel (1:1)
- The proverbs of Solomon (10:1)
- The words of the wise (22:17)
- These also are sayings of the wise (24:23)
- These are other proverbs of Solomon that the officials of King Hezekiah of Judah copied (25:1)
- The words of Agur son of Jakeh (30:1)
- The words of Lemuel, king of Massa, which his mother taught him (31:1, RSV)

Although each of these sections has its own history of compilation and its distinctive motifs, there are common assumptions and emphases. Human beings have a good deal of free choice about the course of their lives, often presented as a choice between two options (the "teaching of the Two Ways"), an emphasis seen in the typical contrasts that form the heart of proverbs — life/death, paths of uprightness/ways of darkness, integrity/perverseness, light/darkness, divine favor/divine punishment, and so on. Humanity is accordingly divided into two groups: righteous/wicked, wise/fools, diligent/slothful, misfortunate/prosperous, rich/poor, the disgraced/the honored, humble/proud, etc.

Proverbs, moreover, suggests that each person gets what he (in light of the male orientation of wisdom literature, the masculine pronoun is justified here) deserves in this life. The righteous prosper and the wicked suffer. Along with this assumption (put to the test in the books of Job and Ecclesiastes), there is a high regard for the pleasures of life — wealth, friends, a good wife, wine, and especially a good reputation. Acting or looking like a fool, conversely, is to be avoided at all costs.

To judge from the contents and several close parallels with older Egyptian wisdom texts, some of the oldest material in the book of Proverbs is contained in chapters 10–22 and 25-29. This material can profitably be contrasted with the later discourses and proverbs in chapters 1–9. A caveat: it is almost impossible to date collections of wisdom literature; the distinction here is simply between earlier and later material.

The older material is less pious and more secular in tone than what we find in chapters 1–9. Evincing a realistic view of life, the older proverbs deflate humbug by the use of common sense and witty or sarcastic remarks (comparable to passages in Job, Ecclesiastes, and some psalms, like Ps. 104). In such texts, God is the creator of the world, but humans have difficulty gaining true knowledge of God and of God's will. People are left to find meaning in their own lives by their own efforts. The good things in life are gained through intelligence and persistence rather than by an individual's piety. The wise man knows that riches might disappear overnight, but he will do everything possible to protect his assets. Prosperity gained through injustice, however, is not good. The pleasures of life are to be enjoyed, but in moderation. Each good, however, has its dangers and its opposites: wine can lead to drunkenness and conversation can turn to gossip. The wise person especially avoids fools (see Prov. 12:15-16; 14:16-18), flatterers, gossips, and contentious people in general. The basis for morality is always self-interest rather than general ideals, religious tradition, or revelation.

> Those who are kind reward themselves,
>> [but]. . . the wicked earn no real gain.   (Prov. 11:17-18)

Later wisdom, examples of which are found in chapters 1–9, by contrast, has a basic theme: "The fear of the LORD is the beginning of knowledge." More inward, more spiritual, with somewhat more sympathy for the poor, the widow, and the orphan, such wisdom is closely connected with faith and morality. No longer is there a great gulf between God and humans, but the personified figure of wisdom — a woman — communicates wisdom directly, similar in form to the oracles uttered by the prophets. The sage is thereby identified with the pious person and is contrasted to scoffers: "The mouth of the righteous brings forth wisdom, but the perverse tongue will be cut off" (10:31). The good things of life are here the results not only of toil and skill but also of the blessing of God. They are divine reward for piety, righteousness, and wisdom (3:14; 8:18; and often).

The distinctiveness of the later collections appears also and especially in a new and startling development: already in 1:20-23, personified Wisdom speaks (she is a woman, because the Hebrew word *hokmah* is feminine in gender, as is also the Greek, *sophia*):

> Wisdom cries out in the street;
>> in the squares she raises her voice. . . .
> "How long, O simple ones, will you love being simple?
>> How long will scoffers delight in their scoffing . . . ?"

In a striking passage, 8:22-31, Wisdom addresses humankind in tones of a goddess who was begotten of the Lord before the creation of the world. She was installed or appointed by God either to rule or to be an associate with God in ruling. Although the meaning of v. 30 is uncertain, it suggests that Wisdom was a master builder with God in the acts of creation, and that divine Wisdom can be seen in the natural order of earth and sky and all that inhabits them. Moreover, on her own authority Wisdom reveals the way of life, truth, knowledge, justice, and righteousness (8:4), in contrast to Folly, also personified as a woman (9:13-18), who leads to death.

Later Jewish wisdom literature develops a number of themes from the more pious sections of Proverbs, including the personification of Wisdom (Sir. 24; Wis. 8:6).

Job

The universal high regard for the book of Job is due in part to its lofty poetry, in part to the timeless nature of the questions it takes up, and especially to the way this magnificent poet turns traditional wisdom on its head, exhibiting a fierce independence of attitude on the question of the relation of personal suffering and cosmic justice.

Traditional Israelite wisdom (and other parts of the Bible as well) insisted that rewards follow righteous behavior just as surely as disaster comes on the heels of unrighteousness and folly. The man Job, in some of the most irreverent language of the Bible, objects. The book desperately searches for meaning in the midst of personal suffering. Is there a relationship between guilt and suffering, between righteousness and prosperity? Several biblical writers, especially Deuteronomy and the books of Joshua, Judges, Samuel, and Kings, articulated the view that, because God has the prime value of power and the prime virtue of justice, what happens in history and in individual life is willed by God. This perspective, promoted both in the great poetic section of the book by Job's three friends and also in the prose prologue and epilogue, is heatedly questioned in the speeches of Job himself. The structure of the book, therefore, is of crucial importance in its interpretation.

THE STRUCTURE OF THE BOOK

The book of Job consists of a poem of amazing creativity and style (3:1–42:6) placed between a prose prologue (1:1–2:13) and a prose epilogue (42:7-17). The prose sections are an ancient folktale (see Ezek. 14:14, 20) about a sheik, rich in sheep and goats — and as righteous a person as one can imagine. Among the striking differences between the prose and the poetry are the following:

> *The man Job* in the prologue is almost incredibly patient, blessing YHWH in spite of dire misfortune. His patience is rewarded in the epilogue, and his friends are rebuked for having spoken falsely. The poem, in stark contrast, presents Job's bitter complaints against God, and his accusations shock his pious friends. Job brings the brute facts of reality as evidence against the idea that life is fair.
>
> *The testing of Job* in the prose folktale is a kind of heavenly experiment: Will even a good man praise God without hope of reward? In the poem, the focus shifts to Job's inner torment and the question of innocent suffering.

The ending of the folktale is a rather artificial vindication of Job: he receives a great bonus for his troubles (how a replacement family can erase the grief over the loss of the original family, however, is not explained). The poem, filled with grief and anguish, has a provocative and mystifying ending.

Differences of detail: In the folktale Job scrupulously offers sacrifices, while in the poem the priestly, cultic side of religion is absent. And the Hebrew words for God differ: in the folktale the sacred name, YHWH, is used; in the original Hebrew of the poem we find also other terms, like El, Eloah, Elohim, and Shaddai.

The poem, therefore, is the meat of the book, and its structure merits attention. The poem in its present form has two complete cycles of speeches between Job and his three friends (Eliphaz, Bildad, and Zophar, chs. 3–21). The third cycle, however, is broken at mid-point (27:1) by various insertions (like ch. 28, which has no relation to the rest of the dialogue, and the speeches of Elihu, chs. 32–37) and apparent deletions. The speeches of Job's friends convey the traditional Israelite view that, because God is both powerful and just, what happens in life is deserved. Job's speeches, by contrast, contain the anguished protest against conventional thought.

THE PROGRESSION OF THOUGHT IN JOB'S SPEECHES

In the opening soliloquy (ch. 3), Job curses the day of his birth, lamenting that he was not stillborn (vv. 1, 16). This theme continues in chapter 7, where, with sarcasm and irony, Job asserts that his only consolation is that his imminent death will free him from the scrutinizing eye of God: "My days are swifter than a weaver's shuttle. . . . For now I shall lie in the earth; you will seek me, but I shall not be" (vv. 6, 21).

In the middle of the first cycle of dialogue, Job expresses his desire for an "umpire," a mediator who could vindicate him by demonstrating that he is suffering innocently. This hope for a mediator continues:

> O earth, do not cover my blood;
>> let my outcry find no resting place.
> Even now, in fact, my witness is in heaven,
>> and he that vouches for me is on high.   (16:18-19)

The "heavenly witness" cannot be God, because God is already the prosecutor, and the witness is to present Job's case to God. The witness, therefore, is most likely the "umpire" of 9:33 — a member of the heavenly court. This thought continues in a famous passage that is almost impossible to translate (because of the many textual variants and also some rare Hebrew word-forms), Job 19:23-27:

> O that my words were written down!
>> O that they were inscribed in a book! . . .
> For I know that my Redeemer lives,
>> and that at the last he will stand upon the earth;
> and after my skin has been thus destroyed,
>> then in my flesh I shall see God,
> whom I shall see on my side,
>> and my eyes shall behold, and not another.

Job, isolated from tribesmen, acquaintances, kinsfolk, houseguests, servants, wife, and finally from his inner circle of friends, begs for pity from them (19:21), but without result ("Why do you, like God, pursue me . . . ?" v. 22). Job wants his case to be written down so that, even if not until after his death, he can be vindicated. He looks for a vindicator, but who is this "Redeemer" (Hebrew: *go'el*)? Through the intervention of this figure, Job will "see God" (v. 26). It is possible that this thought harks back to the ancient idea that the next of kin to a deceased person takes responsibility for the deceased and his estate. But it is more probable that the poet has in mind the "umpire" of 9:33 and the heavenly "witness" of 16:19. Job's hope for a vindicator is expressed also in other places, for example, 23:2-7.

Finally, after several dozen chapters of sitting on a dung-heap, complaining in bitter anguish, comes the climax of the poem —

YHWH's two lectures to Job out of the whirlwind (38:2–39:30 and 40:6–41:34). But Job gets questions — all of them at first glance patronizing and irrelevant to his situation. Job, consumed with grief, disease, and isolation, is forced to listen to lectures on geology, astronomy, meteorology, and zoology. What does Job know about the foundations of the world, the pregnancy periods of various feral animals and their habits, including the hippopotamus (Behemoth, 40:15) and the crocodile (Leviathan, 41:1)? The tone is ironic, as if God were crushing a moth.

JOB'S FINAL RESPONSE

The crux of the poem is in Job's final response to God, 42:1-6:

> Then Job answered YHWH:
> "I know that you can do all things,
>   and that no purpose of yours can be thwarted.
> 'Who is this that hides counsel without knowledge?'
> Therefore I have uttered what I did not understand,
>   things too wonderful for me which I did not know.
> 'Hear, and I will speak;
>   I will question you, and you declare to me.'
> I had heard of you by the hearing of the ear,
>   but now my eye sees you;
> therefore I despise myself,
>   and repent in dust and ashes."

What did the poet intend by concluding the dialogue in this way? Two kinds of approach are possible:

1. Job repents, regretting his lengthy accusations against God. But why? Among the many explanations: By expecting from God a vindication of his own rectitude, Job had negated God's freedom, relegating God to human finitude. Or God's speeches had pointed to an orderly cosmos, a totality full of sense and harmony, in the context of

which Job must view his life. Or Job repents solely because God appears to him.

2. Other readers think that Job does not repent, but continues his accusations. Such readers insist that Job 42:6 has traditionally been mistranslated into English: The Hebrew word translated "despise myself" (*'em'as*) is really a transitive verb, requiring an object. Moreover, the two nouns usually translated "dust and ashes" can equally well be rendered "mortal clay." The verse, therefore, should be translated, "Because of this, I shudder with sorrow for mortal clay." From this perspective, Job ceases his complaint against God only because, after finally witnessing God and hearing God's lectures, he concludes that there is no explanation for the horrible sufferings that human beings must endure on this earth. The poem of Job thereby remains a lament from start to finish.

The epilogue, the second half of the prose folktale, somewhat dulls the drama of the great poem by presenting an artificial conclusion to the book, suggesting that everything turns out well in the end — despite the anguish that remains for anyone who suffers such horrendous loss.

Ecclesiastes

A delight to all incurable pessimists, the book of Ecclesiastes (in Hebrew, Qoheleth, from "the Teacher" or "the Preacher" in 1:1) shows that not all wisdom literature taught a simple doctrine of success in life. A collection of fragments on such common wisdom motifs as riches, oppression, folly, the wise and the fools, its unity consists more of mood than of form. The main theme is announced already in 1:2:

> Vanity of vanities, says the Teacher,
> vanity of vanities! All is vanity.

All is "vanity" — emptiness, a puff of wind, meaninglessness. Whatever goal a person sets — riches, fame, or anything else — human striving is brought to nothing by the great leveler, death. Human striving, manipulating, networking, and ambition are not worth the effort. "Qoheleth," the Teacher, says that this conclusion is the result of long and varied personal experience. "What happens to the fool will happen to me also; why then have I been so very wise?" (2:15).

Death makes all human distinctions meaningless — vanity. Wise and fool alike die, and then the emptiness of what humans have so energetically striven for becomes apparent. Even more, no one knows whether the death of humans is any different from the death of animals (3:19-21).

What is left for us to do? The answer: enjoy our work and our daily routine and whatever small pleasures are available to us:

> There is nothing better for mortals than to eat and drink, and find enjoyment in their toil. This also, I saw, is from the hand of God; for apart from him who can eat or who can have enjoyment? (2:24-25)

> So I saw that there is nothing better than that all should enjoy their work, for that is their lot; who can bring them to see what will be after them? (3:22)

Consistent with such skepticism, the author acknowledges God but draws scant comfort from this because he (less probably she) considers that God must remain largely unknown to humans:

> All this I have tested by wisdom; I said, "I will be wise," but it was far from me. That which is, is far off, and deep, very deep; who can find it out? (7:23-24)

> When I applied my mind to know wisdom, and to see the business that is done on earth, how one's eyes see sleep neither day nor night, then I saw all the work of God, that no one can find out what is happening under the sun. However much they may toil in seeking, they will not find it out; even though those who are wise claim to know, they cannot find it out. (8:16-17)

> Just as you do not know how the breath comes to the bones in the mother's womb, so you do not know the work of God, who makes everything. (11:5)

The ethical values of the Teacher are similar to those of the book of Proverbs: human beings must choose between good and evil, folly and wisdom, riches and poverty. Whichever course is chosen should be followed in moderation and with full awareness of the folly even of this. In one of the most startling texts of the Bible, the Teacher gives his general advice:

> In my vain life I have seen everything; there are righteous people who perish in their righteousness, and there are wicked people who prolong their life in their evil-doing. Do not be too righteous, and do not act too wise; why should you destroy yourself? Do not be too wicked, and do not be a fool; why should you die before your time? It is good that you should take hold of the one, without letting go of the other; for the one who fears God shall succeed with both. (7:15-18)

Ecclesiastes, then, is not a typical book of the Bible. Written pseudonymously (see 1:1) at some point between 500 and 200 B.C.E., it reflects the jaded views of an aged man (see 12:1-8) who has seen everything and concluded that all human striving is no more than meaningless vanity.

The "Letter of James"

Of all New Testament writings, James is the closest in content to Old Testament wisdom literature and is therefore included in this chapter, even though it has an epistolary address ("James, a servant of God and of the Lord Jesus Christ, to the twelve tribes in the Dispersion. Greetings," Jas. 1:1). Although two of Jesus' 12 apostles were named James, Christian tradition has associated the name here with that of Jesus' brother (referred to in Mark 6:3; Gal. 1:19; 2:9; 1 Cor. 15:7), who kept close ties to the Jewish leadership in Jerusalem and was known as James the Just. His death, deplored by many Jewish leaders, came at the hands of nationalist Jews about 62 C.E. in the agitation that preceded the Jewish-Roman war of 66-73. The date of this document, however, has been estimated at any time between 40 and 100 C.E.

The least theological and the most loosely structured of New Testament writings, the letter is almost entirely ethical or moralistic in content, a kind of early Christian book of virtues or written sermon. In line with the later wisdom tradition, like Ben Sira, the author demonstrates concern for the poor and disenfranchised. The author gives practical exhortations and advice on a variety of issues and contexts. He praises wisdom (1:5; 3:13) and warns against discrimination against the poor (1:9-10; 2:1-7; 5:1-6); the evil of malicious talk (1:19-21, 26; 3:2-12; 4:11-12); temptation (1:12-16); envy, selfish ambition, and hypocrisy (3:16-18; 4:1-3); and the taking of oaths (5:12). Conversely, he encourages solicitude (5:13-20), generosity in giving (1:17-18), care of widows and orphans (1:27), endurance in time of trial (1:2), respect for the Torah (2:8-12), humility before God (4:4-10; 4:13-17), and mercy (2:13). There is a strong call for congruence between faith and works, profession and life (1:22-25; 2:14-26).

The concerns of this document are far removed from much of the rest of the New Testament. James offers practical words for ordinary folk — the danger of gossip, the perils of prosperity, and the blessings that come from people living together in harmony.

Reading Wisdom Literature

The contents of Proverbs, Job, Ecclesiastes, and other wisdom writings in the Old Testament are personal rather than national, existential rather than historical, experiential rather than revealed, and reflect the thinking of the movers and shakers of society rather than the dispossessed and marginal. Later books, like Ben Sira, Wisdom of Solomon, and the early Christian letter of James, to a much greater extent reflect the religious piety that developed over the intervening centuries.

Most wisdom literature of the Old Testament is in the form of Hebrew poetry. Each proverb is generally in two lines that form a contrast ("antithetic parallelism"); the speeches in Job and the reflections in Ecclesiastes likewise are constructed from parallel lines (see Appendix A, below).

A good way to begin the study of wisdom literature is to read the book of Ecclesiastes in one sitting and then the first nine chapters of Proverbs. This will give a sense of the spectrum of pessimism/optimism and the range of proverbial and reflective material in wisdom literature. Notice that the poetry of these books is not attributed to God but seems to be teaching directed by an elder sage to young men. Take note also of the subjects of the smaller units: everyday matters of right and wrong, personal success or failure, and ways of achieving balance and satisfaction in life. Absent are references to historical events — whether past, present, or future — and to typical concerns of priests and prophets.

The book of Job is the magnum opus of wisdom literature. Observe the basic differences between the prose framework of the book and the poetic body (see above), and note the contrasting points of view between the speeches of Job and those of others.

Turn finally to the book of James, noting the concern for the poor and reflections of a lower social class than that of the Old Testament wisdom books.

Wisdom literature appeals to those for whom religion has a primarily didactic or ethical function (rather than, for example, a mystical or redemptive function). Proverbs are accessible, universal, and timeless, and the more reflective writings, like Job and Ecclesiastes, deal with problems pondered by all human beings.

3

Praise, Lament, and Thanksgiving:
Poetry of Worship

Texts and text-fragments of hymns and liturgies from the Jerusalem temple, from synagogues, and from early Christian gatherings have found their way into the Old and New Testaments. Recognizing this fact often provides fresh insight. Included among such materials are not only hymns (see below) but also coronation liturgies, laments, thanksgivings, and, for Christians, christological hymns. Liturgical fragments are also imbedded in other materials — historical reports, prophetic books, and the Gospels and letters of the New Testament (for example, 1 Sam. 2:1-10; 2 Sam. 22:2-51; 1 Chr. 16:8-36; Hab. 3:2-19; see also below).

The Psalms: Worship Book of the Temple

Until the 20th century, most readers assumed that the Psalms were written by David and other Israelite heroes, and that they reflected crucial episodes in their individual lives. This view was based on the titles found at the beginning of many of the psalms.

In the first half of the 20th century a new approach to the Psalms was pioneered by European scholars, who showed that most psalms were composed as liturgies — for public worship in the temple at Jerusalem or for individual prayer. (Scholars differ on the question whether more psalms were originally composed for the First Temple, built by Solomon around 950 and destroyed by the Babylonians in 587 B.C.E., or the Second Temple, begun around 515 B.C.E.) Five major types of psalms were identified:

1. The *hymn* is a poem of which the sole purpose is to extol the glory and wonders of God. The emotional state of the worshiper is not suggested. Hymns might focus on the majesty of God as seen in nature (Pss. 8; 24), in history (Pss. 113–118, esp. 114), in the temple at Jerusalem (Pss. 84; 122), or of YHWH as enthroned as king of Zion (Pss. 24; 47). Psalm 29, possibly derived from a Canaanite poem, is a good example of a hymn. Between a symmetrical prologue (vv. 1-2) and epilogue (vv. 10-11) are four strophes (stanzas) that describe a powerful thunderstorm, with lightning, thunder, and hail, moving from the Mediterranean (v. 3) south to the wilderness of Kadesh (v. 8) where it dies. The writer's focus, however, is on the response of the worshipers in the temple, who, sensing the power of God in the storm, cry, "Glory" (Hebrew: *kabod*).

2. The *national lament* has a typical form: the occasion for the lament is followed by the plea, "How long, O YHWH?" or "Why?" An appeal to the blessings of God in the past and an oracle of comfort or assurance conclude the lament. The purpose of the lament is to move God to pity and to action.

Laments are found in the Bible apart from the Psalms. The book of Joel is a national lament occasioned by a devastating plague of locusts, while the book of Lamentations mourns over the fall of Jerusalem to the Babylonians on the 9th of Ab (Jewish calendar) in 587 B.C.E. Lamentations combines intense emotion with a highly developed poetic structure. The first four of its five poems (corresponding to the chapter divisions in English translations) are acrostics (the first letter of each verse or strophe follows the sequence of the Hebrew alphabet). Technically considered, the fifth poem is a national lament, the third an individual lament, and the first, second, and fourth poems funeral dirges. The poems convey a harsh reality: carnage, destruction, cannibalism, slaughter, almost unspeakable anguish. How could the fall of Jerusalem be reconciled with faith in the God who had entered into covenant with Moses? Can God be the source of horror? Had God deserted the people? In spite of this anguish, the whole is a kind of prayer aimed at evoking God's mercy and intervention.

Within the Psalter, Psalm 137 ("By the waters of Babylon — there we sat down and there we wept/when we remembered Zion . . .") expresses all the extreme emotion of this genre in recalling the beginning of exile. Quite different is the mood in the great Psalm 90, which reflects on the brevity and harshness of life:

> Lord, you have been our dwelling place
> in all generations.
> Before the mountains were brought forth,
> or ever you had formed the earth and the world,
> from everlasting to everlasting you are God.
> You turn us back to dust,
> and say, "Turn back, you mortals."
> For a thousand years in your sight
> are like yesterday when it is past,
> or like a watch in the night.
> You sweep them away; they are like a dream,
> like grass that is renewed in the morning;
> in the morning it flourishes and is renewed;
> in the evening it fades and withers.

3. Most numerous in the book of Psalms are the *individual laments*, which are similar in form to the communal laments and in content to the speeches of Job. While the occasions for laments vary, a significant group stems from those who feel falsely accused and see themselves as objects of calumny. Most of these psalm writers convey no consciousness of sin, guilt, or shortcoming. Like Job, they were proud of their integrity and certain that they were suffering unjustly. They therefore appealed to the justice of God, at times leaving room for imprecations and prayers for vengeance (Pss. 5; 55; 58; 69; and 83). A few, like 42 and 43, are noble supplications in which the occasion for the lament is not clearly indicated.

In some respects, the most impressive of the individual laments are the only two that center on repentance, Psalms 51 and 130, both of which continue to be used liturgically to the present day.

Psalm 22, a vivid account of a tortured individual, is heavily cited by New Testament writers in their descriptions of Jesus' crucifixion. Such usage has to do with the finding of parallels rather than the fulfillment of predictions.

The large number of individual laments in comparison with the number of hymns shows the human tendency to beg and complain more than to praise.

4. *Royal psalms* center on the king and were used as coronation liturgies. The king in Jerusalem could be called the "son" of the Almighty (Ps. 2:7), and his rule could be said to make amends for the injustices and weaknesses of society, bringing life and prosperity to the earth.

Psalm 2 opens with the plotting of Judah's neighbors, intent on taking advantage of the interregnum. The psalmist, however, looks to heaven, where YHWH laughs derisively and announces the new king in Zion. The king then speaks of his commission from God, promising sudden destruction of the plotters.

Psalm 110 likewise refers to YHWH's commissioning and the king's military prowess:

> YHWH says to my lord,
>   "Sit at my right hand
> until I make your enemies your footstool."
> . . . .
> YHWH is at your right hand;
>   he will shatter kings on the day of his wrath.
> He will execute judgment among the nations,
>   filling them with corpses;
> he will shatter heads
>   over the wide earth.

After the Israelite monarchies were brought to an end in 587 B.C.E., these magnificent poems gradually came to be interpreted as referring to the future restoration of the Davidic monarchy, that is, to a royal Messiah. These psalms, especially Psalm 110, are cited in this sense in the New Testament.

5. *Thanksgivings* are liturgies for personal or communal use. Included here are some familiar texts, like Psalms 23 ("The LORD is my shepherd, I shall not want") and 103 ("Bless the LORD, O my soul, and all that is within me, bless his holy name").

Among the "minor" types are wisdom psalms (including Pss. 1; 37; 49; 53; 112; and 128), songs sung by pilgrims on their way to a festival in Jerusalem (Ps. 84, "How lovely is your dwelling place, O LORD of hosts!"; Ps. 121, "I lift up my eyes to the hills, from where will my help come?"; and Ps. 122, "I was glad when they said to me, 'Let us go to the house of the LORD!'"), and songs of trust.

Christian Hymns and Other Liturgical Texts

The first Christians worshiped with other Jews at the temple in Jerusalem (Acts 2:46; 5:12, 42; and often) but also in private homes, which became the pattern for Christian groups in other places. For such gatherings, a variety of worship materials was needed: hymns, supplications, prayers at the "Lord's Supper," baptismal formulas, and so on. Hymns, hymn fragments, and other worship texts can be detected in several New Testament books. The first two chapters of the Gospel of Luke have several such poetic texts, including the "Song of Mary" or "Magnificat" (Luke 1:46-55), the "Song of Zechariah" (1:68-79), and the "Song of Simeon" (2:29-32) — all of which have strong Old Testament allusions. In the book of Revelation, fragments of early Christian hymns and other poetry of worship can be seen in 4:8, 11; 5:9-10, 12, 13; 7:12, 15-17; 11:15, 17-18; 12:10-12; 15:3-4; 19:1-3, 5, 6-8; and 21:3-4. Other possible remnants of Christian worship materials are Matt. 11:28-30; 28:19; 1 Cor. 11:23-26; Eph. 4:8; 5:14; 1 Tim. 2:5; 3:16; and 2 Tim. 2:11-13.

Jesus as the Christ (Messiah) of God came to be the object of liturgical veneration in many Christian groups, especially outside of Jerusalem. Such texts may be imbedded in various New Testament writings, in particular two early Christian letters, Philippians and Colossians.

In encouraging Philippian believers to cultivate the virtues of love, patience, and humility, Paul cites what might well be an early Christian hymn in poetic form that refers to the preexistent Christ,

> Who, though he was in the form of God,
>> did not regard equality with God
>> as something to be exploited,
> but emptied himself,
>> taking the form of a slave,
>> being born in human likeness.
> And being found in human form,
>> he humbled himself
>> and became obedient to the point of death —
>> even death on a cross.
> Therefore God also highly exalted him
>> and gave him the name
>> that is above every name,
> so that at the name of Jesus
>> every knee should bend,
>> in heaven and on earth and under the earth,
> and every tongue should confess
>> that Jesus Christ is Lord,
>> to the glory of God the Father. (Phil. 2:6-11)

The focus in this poem is not on what Jesus taught or did during his activity in Galilee and Judea but rather on the pattern of humiliation→exaltation found in some Old Testament texts (especially Isa. 52:13–53:12). Emphasized are his preexistence with God, his entering into human life as a servant, his humiliating death, and his subsequent exaltation by God. Similar liturgical use (perhaps as a recited creed) might lie behind Col. 1:15-20.

The wording of the Lord's Prayer in Matthew (6:9-13), when compared with Luke's version (11:2-4), also shows signs of liturgical adaptation. (The prayer is found also in the early Christian writing *Didache* 8:2.) Luke does not have the petitions "your will be done" and "deliver us from evil"; he has the simple address "Father" (Matthew: "Our Father") and also in other ways reflects a shorter form. The many textual variants at the end of Matthew's prayer (the doxology) also demonstrate that the Matthean version was used by Christians in worship. Perhaps not surprisingly, the prayer in all its details can be read as a good Jewish prayer of the time, even as it fits the general tenor of Jesus' teaching.

Matthew concludes his Gospel with an announcement of the risen Jesus that includes a liturgical baptismal formula: "baptizing them in the name of the Father and of the Son and of the Holy Spirit . . . (28:19). This tripartite formula might well be a development that replaced baptism in the name of Jesus alone (see Acts 19:5; Rom. 6:3; 1 Cor. 1:13).

Early Christians also used in their celebration of "the Lord's Supper" some version of a text now found in Matt. 26:26-29; Mark 14:22-25; Luke 22:14-20; and 1 Cor. 11:24-25, which centers on the words of Jesus about the bread and wine and points ahead to fellowship in the kingdom of God.

Recognizing and Reading
Liturgical Material

The liturgical origin of the books of Psalms, Lamentations, and Joel is almost certain. To identify other ancient texts that have a cultic origin requires knowledge of the function and nature of worship practices — knowledge that, because of the sparseness of available sources, often remains sketchy. Even so, reading a specific text with this possible origin in mind can be a hedge against unhelpful approaches and can often provide fresh insight into and interest in texts that otherwise might appear vacuous.

Partly because of numerous allusions to the Psalms in the New Testament, especially in the narratives of Jesus' death, Christians have traditionally read many of the Psalms "christologically," that is, as pointing to Jesus in some way. Such an approach contradicts the basic principle that a text must have had meaning to its original author and readers — to say nothing of the original liturgical function of the Psalms. Early Christians naturally found parallels between the individual laments and the royal psalms, on the one hand, and the fate of Jesus, on the other. But the setting of the Psalms in ancient Israel cannot be ignored. A good first step is to read several psalms of different genres with a view toward determining their setting in ancient worship.

Most liturgical material in the Bible as a whole comes to us in poetic form (see below, Appendix A). Poetic fragments imbedded in letters, Gospels, or historical reports, often have a liturgical origin. The reader can observe whether the text reflects a group (does it use the first person plural?) or serves the purpose of an obvious cultic practice, for example, national lament among the Israelites or baptism or the Lord's Supper among the Christians.

The Psalms have been and are universally admired by Jews and Christians and have brought comfort to many individuals in time of trouble, often without regard to the liturgical origin of the texts. In general, however, a preoccupation with liturgical materials appeals to persons who seek regularity, dignity, and predictability in worship. Contrasts with other types of literature in the Old Testament are apparent. Few wisdom teachers aspired to become liturgical experts and, although some prophets had a priestly ancestry, the prophetic tradition of Israel functioned as an ongoing critique of piety that remained formal and external. Such differences are reflected also in the varieties of Christian worship even today.

4

The Appeal to the Past: Historical and Quasi-Historical Narratives

Biblical traditions about persons or events of the past circulated in several stages in antiquity, including preliterary (oral) forms, short written accounts, and epic literature.

Preliterary narrative materials now incorporated into biblical epics include legends and lore about tribal heroes, war songs, explanations of the origin of names and customs (etiologies), group relationships, genealogies, and much else. Ancient Israelites, like the early Christians, had a flourishing oral narrative tradition, some of which eventually came to be put into writing.

The Old Testament itself gives evidence of early writings about events. The lost "Book of Jashar" (Book of the Upright), a collection of poetry recounting exploits of Israel's heroes, is twice mentioned, once in connection with a battle between Israelites and the "Amorites" or Canaanites (Josh. 10:13) and again regarding David's lament over the deaths of Saul and Jonathan (2 Sam. 1:18). Another book of battle poetry was the "Book of the Wars of YHWH" (Num. 21:14-15). Other early poetry includes songs of triumph such as the "Song of Miriam" (Exod. 15:21) and the "Song of Moses" (Exod. 15:1-18), the present context of which is the overthrow of the Egyptian army at the Red Sea ("Sea of Reeds"). Israelite versions of common motifs, like creation and the flood, circulated from early times in biblical history, as did stories

34

about common ancestors and tribal exploits. Moreover, accounts of a king's activities were customarily drawn up at the conclusion of his reign ("The Book of the Acts of Solomon," 1 Kgs. 11:41; "Book of the Annals of the Kings of Judah," 1 Kgs. 14:19, 29; etc.).

From such early oral and written threads large epics were eventually woven. Over a long period of time (several centuries), these epics were edited to form the grand narrative in the Bible, a story that begins with creation and then centers on the figure of Abraham, the exodus from Egypt, the conquest of Canaan, the period of the judges, the time of the kings, the end of the Israelite kingdoms and Babylonian exile, and the postexilic reconstruction. The books of the Apocrypha form a bridge between the Old Testament and the New, although with considerable gaps. The first of the New Testament writings are the letters of Paul, with the Gospels and other writings following fairly closely behind.

In all cases, the historical and quasi-historical writings have a retrospective function. They interpret the past from the perspective of the authors' present. The epic in the books Joshua through 2 Kings recounts the history of Israel in its own land from the perspective of Babylonian exile. And the Gospels tell the story of Jesus from the perspective of issues of two or three generations later.

The story in a nutshell has the following shape:

Prehistory:	Creation, flood, Abraham (who is dated by some to the middle of the Middle Bronze Age, ca. 2000-1750 B.C.E.)
1290 B.C.E.:	Exodus from Egypt
1250-1000 B.C.E.:	Israelite conquest of Canaan; the "judges"
1000-922 B.C.E.:	Reign of King David, 1000-961, and of King Solomon, 961-922
922-722 B.C.E.:	Northern Kingdom, Israel; destroyed by Assyria in 722; Elijah, ca. 855; Amos, ca. 750
922-587 B.C.E.:	Southern Kingdom, Judah; destroyed by Babylon in 587; Isaiah, 742–ca. 687; Jeremiah, 627–ca. 580; Ezekiel, ca. 600-580
587-538 B.C.E.:	Babylonian exile; release granted after the conquest

of Babylon by the Persian Cyrus the Great; Second
Isaiah, ca. 538

538-450 B.C.E.: Reconstruction in Judea; Second Temple dedicated,
516; Ezra and Nehemiah

332 B.C.E.: Conquest of Palestine by Alexander the Great, beginning of the Hellenistic period

167 B.C.E.: Beginning of the Maccabean period, leading to an
independent Jewish state

63 B.C.E.: Beginning of Roman rule of Palestine

37-4 B.C.E.: Reign of Herod the Great

29-30 C.E.: Activity of John the Baptist and Jesus

35-62 C.E.: Missionary activity of Paul; his letters, 50-62

66-73 C.E.: Jewish-Roman War; fall of Jerusalem, August 70

Prehistory: From Paradise to Egypt in Genesis

The first part of the biblical epic, the book of Genesis, recounts events and
persons from the mists of prehistory. As a whole, but especially for chapters
1–11 ("primeval history"), these materials do not lend themselves to historical assessment. Genesis is an edited record of ancient Israelite traditions regarding origins — the origins of the world and its inhabitants and also the
origin of the people of Israel and their relationships to other peoples.

Scholars have detected at least three major written sources that un-
derlie the present narrative of Genesis, Exodus, and Numbers. The earliest of these sources, commonly known as "J" (the "Yahwist," German
"Jahwist," because it uses the divine name YHWH from the beginning),
could have been put into writing in the early part of the monarchy, the
10th century B.C.E. Traditions from Israel's northern tribes, "E" (the
"Elohist," from the generic Hebrew *elohim,* "God," because it generally
avoids using the personal name YHWH until it is revealed to Moses in
the book of Exodus), are noticeable in texts beginning in Genesis 15. A
later source, "P," reflects priestly traditions edited as late as or later than
the Babylonian exile (6th century B.C.E.). Like E, P avoids using the
name YHWH until it is revealed to Moses.

Most English versions of the Bible render the Hebrew name YHWH as "the LORD" (capital letters), which makes it possible to identify the J material in Genesis. Differences of style and content distinguish E from P in Genesis — and all sources from each other after the divine name begins to be used in Exodus. Evident in Gen. 1:1–2:4a (P) is a symmetry between "days" 1-3 and days 4-6, a cosmic scope, and the formal language, compared with the earthy description of the separate creation of man and woman and the poignant and intriguing story of paradise lost in 2:4b–4:26. The priestly continuation in chapters 5 and 11 offers a linear genealogy with chronology that leads to the story of the Hebrew patriarch Abraham. In between, chapters 6–9 are a conflation of J and P on the great flood.

The patriarchal narratives, Genesis 12–50, are structured by the special arrangement ("covenant") between God, on the one side, and Abraham and his descendants, on the other (12:1-3; 15:7-21; 17:1-14). This "Abrahamic" covenant centers on the promise of land and descendants and on the rite of circumcision. The biblical narrative then proceeds through Abraham's son Isaac to the marvelous Joseph stories (Gen. 37–50), which give a narrative explanation for the family of Jacob moving to Egypt, setting the stage for the great redemptive act of the epic, the exodus of Israel from Egypt.

Exodus and Conquest:
Exodus, Numbers, Joshua, Judges

EXODUS

The narrative of the exodus of the Israelites from Egypt centers on

1. The birth and call of Moses (Exod. 1–4), which took place after "a new king arose over Egypt, who did not know Joseph" (1:8), and when the Egyptian capital was located in the delta region. This fits the 19th Dynasty (1308-1207 B.C.E.), especially its second king, Rameses II (1290-1224), who is the most likely candidate to have

been the pharaoh of the exodus. Striking in these chapters is the theophany (manifestation of God) of the burning bush (ch. 3), in which the personal name of God, YHWH, is revealed to Moses (3:13-15; see also 6:2). From this point on, all epic sources use this divine name.

2. The narrative of the 10 plagues (Exod. 7–11) results from a conflation of J, E, and P. It culminates in an etiology of the origin of Passover (ch. 12).

3. The crossing of the sea (Exod. 14–15) was central to the Israelite memory of the exodus. Chapter 14 gives a prose account, while a brief "Song of Miriam" (15:21) and the lengthier "Song of Moses" (15:1-18) are in poetic form. This event is situated at the "Sea of Reeds" (the traditional translation "Red Sea" in 15:4, 22 is influenced by the Greek versions), which cannot be more precisely located than in an area generally southeast of the delta region.

4. The making of the covenant between YHWH and Moses (and all Israel) at the holy mountain (Sinai or Horeb) (Exod. 19–24) came to be the single most important memory and event in Israelite and subsequent Jewish history and thought, determinative for religious identity. In Exodus 19, one of the most majestic of biblical theophanies, YHWH personally approaches Israel in "a dense cloud" (v. 9), with thunder, lightning, and continuing trumpet blasts. YHWH descends in fire upon the mountain to speak to Moses the words of the covenant (Exod. 20–23, including the Ten Commandments, 20:3-17). The covenant and laws are "ratified" in a sacrifice described in Exodus 24, with references to the "blood of the covenant" and the "book of the covenant." The Mosaic covenant and the "Law of Moses" are seen as the birth of the nation of Israel (Exod. 19:6; see also Exod. 4:22-23) and the origin of the Israelite worship system (ark of the covenant, priesthood, sacrificial system, the tabernacle as precursor of the temple).

NUMBERS

Literary unity in the book of Numbers, a collection of materials from J, E, P, and elsewhere, is lacking. Its narratives, which follow the adventures of Israel from the last days at Mount Sinai to their encampment in the plains of Moab (across the Jordan from the "promised land") are found in chapters 11–14; 20–25; and 31. Among these narratives are included a first attempt at the conquest of Palestine (chs. 13–14), punishment for its failure, and revolts against Moses (ch. 16). A long stay at Kadesh (the final edition of the book presupposes something like 35 years) ends in chapter 20, when the people move to Mount Hor on the edge of Edom (chs. 20–22). Then the plains of Moab (22:1) are the setting for some of the most eloquent of ancient Israelite poetry, the oracles of Balaam, a holy man of Mesopotamia (narrative, chs. 22–24; oracles, 23:18-24; 24:3-9; 24:15-24). Additional narratives are the apostasy in Moab (ch. 25), the appointment of Joshua as Moses' successor (27:12-23), a holy war against Midian, and the appointment of cities of refuge in the yet-unconquered promised land (ch. 35).

THE "DEUTERONOMIC HISTORY"

The books Joshua, Judges, 1-2 Samuel, and 1-2 Kings present a narrative that begins with the entry of Israel into the promised land and ends with the exile of the people from this land, a story that encompasses several centuries, approximately 1250 to 580 B.C.E. Editorial material in each of these books, heavily influenced by the thought of the book of Deuteronomy (see below, Chapter 6), contains dire warnings against idolatry and the proliferation of cult centers. It is not difficult to distinguish the editorial interpretation from the earlier narratives, even though the latter present historical difficulties. As a whole, the macro narrative is a gripping and fascinating tragedy.

JOSHUA

The initial conquest of Palestine is described in Joshua as a series of liturgical (chs. 3–5) and military (chs. 6–11) events. Forays are made into the central hill country (chs. 6–9), including Ai and Gibeon; into the southern hill country (ch. 10); and into the north (ch. 11), which included a decisive victory at Hazor, a major Canaanite city. Editorial comments to the effect that "Joshua defeated the whole land, the hill country and the Negeb and the lowland and the slopes, and all their kings" (10:40; see 11:16-23) are qualified by lists of sites that the Israelites were unable to conquer at that time (13:13; 15:63; 16:10; 17:12-13) as well as by the picture in the book of Judges of ongoing battles against the Canaanites and other neighbors.

Joshua 24, a narrative that bristles with difficulties and intrigue, tells of a gathering of the Israelite tribes at Shechem, a city not mentioned in early chapters as having been captured. There Joshua, after rehearsing the history of Israel from Abraham to the conquest, challenged the assembly to choose between the worship of YHWH and the tribal gods of the ancestors beyond the Euphrates River (24:14). The people chose YHWH. This narrative presupposes that the Israelite ancestors were polytheists: "Long ago your ancestors — Terah and his sons Abraham and Nahor — lived beyond the Euphrates and served other gods" (24:2). It presupposes also that some of Joshua's audience were not exclusive worshipers of YHWH and had not participated in the exodus events. Moreover, some extrabiblical evidence suggests that the residents of Shechem felt themselves kin of the invading Israelites. What may be happening at the gathering at Shechem, therefore, is the absorption of Hebrews from groups descended from collateral lines compared with the invaders. For these people, Joshua also "made statutes and ordinances . . . at Shechem" (24:25).

JUDGES

The book of Judges incorporates stories of Israel's ancient heroes into a schema that centers on the clash of religions — YHWHism against the religion of the Canaanites ("Baalism") or the Philistines (their chief god was Dagon). The introduction (2:6–3:6) and the editorial comments that link one story to another are a simple form of the idea of rewards and punishments that is articulated in the book of Deuteronomy. When the Israelites are faithful to YHWH, they are free and prosperous; when they engage in foreign cults, they are given into the hands of their enemies. The stories are set in the period between Joshua and Saul, that is, approximately the 12th and 11th centuries B.C.E.

The term "judge" is applied to early tribal heroes in the sense that they defended the righteous cause by engaging in military action against oppressors. Judges whose activities are given more than a passing notice are Ehud, Deborah, Gideon, Jephthah, and Samson. Masterful tales in themselves, they reflect a violent period that culminated in the ascendancy of the Philistines, a non-Semitic people who settled on the southern Palestinian coast. Chapters 17–21 describe a time of anarchy and tribal migration, when "all the people did what was right in their own eyes" (21:25).

The Monarchy:
The Books of Samuel and Kings

The books of Samuel and Kings are not only remarkable literary achievements but also historical sources of great importance, describing the four centuries during which the Israelites lived under a monarchy. The text can be considered in six steps.

1. The origin of the monarchy (narrated in 1 Sam. 1–12) is a response of the Israelites to the threat from the Philistines who, by the end of the 11th century, had garrisons throughout the area of Israelite settlement and who had begun to use iron in addition to bronze (1 Sam. 13:19-21). After a disastrous Israelite defeat at the "battle of Ebenezer," the prophet-judge Samuel anointed Saul as king. The editors of 1 Samuel appear to have used two different sources to describe this momentous change (compare 9:1–10:16; 11 with 7–8; 10:17-27; 12).

2. Saul's reign (1 Sam. 13–31) is a classic tragedy, compounded by

the machinations of Samuel. Saul was caught between the old order of charismatic judges and the new hereditary monarchy. After Saul's considerable success in stemming Philistine encroachments, Samuel accused Saul of breaking the rules of holy war in a battle with the Amalekites (ch. 15), the result of which was the rejection of Saul by Samuel and — so the text asserts — by YHWH as well. The climax of this tragedy is given in 1 Samuel 28 and 31, with Saul's death on Mount Gilboa in the northern hill country after a battle with the Philistines.

3. David, next to Moses, was remembered as the greatest of Israel's heroes. His long reign (approximately 1000-960 B.C.E.) is described in one of the finest literary and historical pieces of antiquity, 2 Samuel, especially chapters 9–20. Essentially a throne succession story, 2 Samuel provides ample evidence of David's astounding military achievements, administrative shrewdness, political savvy, and religious piety. It is therefore all the more amazing that the text includes also the sordid aspects of David's reign — his adultery with Bathsheba; political executions; and rape, murder, and rebellion among his children. David's court prophet, Nathan, represents in this story the ideals of justice and personal morality. (The parallel account of David's reign in 1 Chronicles has no mention of these lapses.)

4. The reign of Solomon (approximately 960-922 B.C.E.), son of David, is described in 1 Kings 1–11 as a time when the Israelite kingdom became a small empire, with magnificent building projects, international diplomacy, and peace. The editors' interest centers on one project, the building of the temple in Jerusalem, where an elaborate priesthood oversaw royal worship and the sacrificial system. (This temple was burned by the Babylonians in 587.) The editors also provide several narratives that illustrate Solomon's proverbial wisdom. The final evaluation of his reign (1 Kgs. 11), however, is negative: Solomon entered into political marriage with a number of foreign wives, whom he allowed to continue to practice their native religions in Jerusalem. The editors find in this the main cause of the division of the kingdom at Solomon's death. Alongside of this, however, we read that Solomon, to support his ambitious building program, had created a massive system of

forced labor and had imposed on his subjects heavy levies and taxes. The revolt came from the northern tribes, instigated by Jeroboam, who had been a foreman in Solomon's labor camps.

5. The Divided Monarchy: Upon Solomon's death in 922 B.C.E., the northern tribes rejected rule from Jerusalem and set up a separate kingdom, Israel. The history of the two kingdoms, Israel and Judah, is recounted in 1 Kings 12–2 Kings 25. In this material, a judgment on every king in both kingdoms is given with the mention of his death. Derived from the book of Deuteronomy, the two major criteria for these evaluations are whether (1) the king fostered Jerusalem as the exclusive site for sacrifice to YHWH and (2) he took measures to exclude the worship of deities other than YHWH. Because the northern kingdom set up rival shrines to that of Jerusalem, each king in the north is condemned. Only the second criterion is used to evaluate the kings of Judah, of which only two, Hezekiah and Josiah, are praised without qualification; six are given moderate praise, and 10 are said to have done "what was evil in the sight of YHWH."

Of the 19 kings of Israel, several are noteworthy: Omri (876-869; 1 Kgs. 16:21-28), who built Samaria as his capital and began a policy of cooperation with the Phoenicians; his son Ahab (869-850; 1 Kgs. 16:28–22:40), under whom Israel witnessed a clash fostered by the prophet Elijah between the Canaanite-Phoenician cult of Baal and that of YHWH; Jehu (842-815; 2 Kgs. 10:1-36), who slaughtered the priests of Baal; and Jeroboam II (786-746; 2 Kgs. 14:23-29), the last successful king of Israel, whose policies were reproached by the prophets Amos and Hosea. In 722 B.C.E. the northern kingdom was brought to an end by the invasion of Assyria.

Judah, the smaller kingdom, more isolated and less fertile than Israel, retained the Davidic dynasty and the centrality of the Jerusalem temple throughout its history. Among its kings were Ahaz (735-715; 2 Kgs. 16), who witnessed the end of the sister kingdom; Hezekiah (715-687; 2 Kgs. 18–20), who withstood Assyrian threats and reformed the state religion; Manasseh (687-642, 2 Kgs. 21:1-18), who willingly accepted Assyrian hegemony; and Josiah (640-609; 2 Kgs. 22:1–23:30), who rapidly reasserted Israelite traditions and promulgated a religious reform prompted by the discovery in the temple of a law book, most probably a form of Deuteronomy. Among prophets active in the southern kingdom were Isaiah (742-687), Micah (approximately 710), Nahum (approximately 615), Huldah (2 Kgs. 22:14), Zephaniah (approximately 610), Habbakuk (approximately 600), and Jeremiah (active 627-580). Ezekiel, a Jerusalem priest, was taken to Babylon in 598 and remained active there for several years.

6. The fall of Jerusalem to the Babylonians in August 587 B.C.E. is the great watershed event of Old Testament history. The story is recounted in 2 Kings 24–25 and, in more detail, in Jeremiah 27; 32–45 (this includes the poignant narrative of the last years of Jeremiah); 52. By 605 the Babylonians under Nebuchadnezzar had established themselves as the dominant power in the Near East; they captured Jerusalem in 598. When Zedekiah, who had been installed in Jerusalem by Nebuchadnezzar, renounced allegiance to Babylon, the Babylonians returned, devastated the country, and besieged Jerusalem. When the city fell, the temple was destroyed, the leaders exiled to Babylon, and the nation came to an abrupt end.

This turning point radically affected Jewish life, thought, literature, and culture. Jerusalem priests, now in Babylon, had to show how the worship of YHWH could continue in exile. Identifying marks of Jewishness now centered on circumcision (commanded in Gen. 17:9-14), the Sabbath (articulated in Gen. 2:1-3), and memories of the past, including the traditions gathered around Moses and David, now preserved in writing. Prophetic oracles kept alive the hope of return to the Holy Land and of the restoration of the line of David ("messianism"). Eventually there arose also a new literary genre, apocalyptic literature, which looked for the destruction of the present age and the establishment of a universal kingdom of justice and peace (see Chapter 7, below).

The Reconstruction:
The Books of Ezra and Nehemiah

Two clusters of events dominate Old Testament history after the end of the nation in 587 B.C.E.: the rebuilding of Judea (as Judah now comes to be known) and the Maccabean (Hasmonean) revolt.

THE REBUILDING OF JUDEA

Although the editing of the books of Ezra and Nehemiah has resulted in much confusion, with conflated individuals and the same person's work described in parts of both books, the outline of the story they narrate is fairly clear. Jewish hopes rose when Babylon fell to Cyrus the Great of Persia in October 539 B.C.E. In line with his policy that conquered people should continue their own cults in their ancestral homelands, Cyrus issued a decree in 538 that ordered the restoration of the Jewish community and cultic system in Palestine. This decree is preserved in Ezra 1:2-4 (= 2 Chr. 36:22-23) and, in the Aramaic language, in Ezra 6:3-5. (As noted in Chapter 5, below, Cyrus is mentioned by name in Second Isaiah.)

The first return of Jews from Babylon to Judea involved about 50 thousand persons (Ezra 2:64) under a "prince," Sheshbazzar (Ezra 1:8; 5:14). Work on building the temple did not begin until approximately 521 B.C.E. (Ezra 5:16). More progress came under Sheshbazzar's successor, Zerubbabel, a descendant of the line of David. He, along with the prophets Haggai and Zechariah and the priest Joshua, enabled work to proceed so that a dedication was celebrated in March 515 (Ezra 6:13-18).

Nehemiah's activity in Jerusalem took place around 445 B.C.E. In an amazingly short time, he succeeded in gaining for Judea increased political stability and oversaw the building of the walls of Jerusalem (Neh. 6:15). He took strong measures to exclude aliens from the new province, dissolving mixed marriages (Neh. 13:23-27).

Ezra, of priestly ancestry, "a scribe skilled in the law of Moses" (Neh.

12:1; Ezra 7:6, 11, 12, 21), set for himself a limited task: to reorganize the religious worship of the temple as a self-preservation measure. He did this in two ways: (1) Ezra brought with him from Babylon to Jerusalem "the book of the law of Moses" (Neh. 8:1), gathered the people and, for seven days, read the book to them. Although the identity of this "book" cannot be known (the Pentateuch or a part of it?), the Torah ("law," "instruction") was now accepted as authoritative for Judea. (2) Ezra emphasized the importance of genealogical purity in the nation (see Ezra 9:1-2), which involved not only the demonstration of continuity between preexilic and postexilic times but also the prohibition of marriages with non-Judeans. The date of Ezra's work in Jerusalem must remain uncertain, but a date shortly after 400 B.C.E. is possible.

THE MACCABEAN REVOLT

Written sources for events in Jerusalem between Ezra (approximately 400 B.C.E.) and the Maccabean revolt (around 170) are scanty, except for the conquests of Alexander the Great (he captured Palestine in 332).

First Maccabees is an important source for our knowledge of the revolt, superior in several respects to 2 Maccabees, which carries the story further (both books are in the so-called Apocrypha). In addition, the apocalyptic book of Daniel, written at an early point during the revolt, provides important information, although in obscure symbolic form.

First Maccabees opens with the mention of Alexander the Great (1:1-4), one of the great military leaders of human history. In a short period of time, Alexander defeated the Persians in a series of battles, gaining control over an area from Greece to Egypt to India. Alexander died in 323 B.C.E. at the age of 33. This began the "Hellenistic Age," during which Greek language and culture came to be disseminated throughout the known world of the time. The dominance of Greek ways, however, led in Judea to a clash with Jewish piety, based as it was on the "Law of Moses."

Antiochus IV "Epiphanes" (ruled 175-164 B.C.E.), a Syrian successor of Alexander, encouraged Greek practices in Jerusalem. By 167 he determined that all people in his kingdom "should be one . . . and give up their particular customs" (1 Macc. 1:41-42). The practice of circumcision — the initiation rite of Judaism — and possession of books of the Law were punished by death. But the last straw came on the 15th day of the month of Chislev, when the Syrians "erected a desolating sacrilege" (sometimes translated "abomination of desolation") on the altar of burnt offering at the temple in Jerusalem (1 Macc. 1:54). This was apparently an altar to the Greek god Zeus. The temple was now unfit for Jewish worship, and the religious practice of Judaism a capital offense.

Jewish revolt began in the small town of Modein, 17 miles northwest of Jerusalem, led by an aged priest, Mattathias, and his five sons (1 Macc. 2). (They were of the house of Hasmon; hence the more official name of the family, Hasmonean. The term "Maccabee" was a nickname applied to the oldest son, Judas.) Almost miraculously, Judas and his troops were able in 167 B.C.E. to gain control of the temple area in Jerusalem. They cleansed the sanctuary, now in disrepair, and, three years to the day after its pollution, resumed sacrifices there (1 Macc. 4:38-58). This is commemorated in the annual festival of Hanukkah (v. 59).

Judas led the struggle until his death in 160. His brother Jonathan followed (160-143), then his brother Simon (142-134), then Simon's son John Hyrcanus (134-104). After a period of increasing inner-Jewish strife, the Roman general Pompey brought Palestine under Roman rule, ending the period of Jewish independence. Rome appointed Herod "the Great" King of the Jews in 37 B.C.E. He died in 4 B.C.E., shortly after the birth of Jesus, according to Matthew and Luke.

The Rise of Christianity:
The Book of Acts

The book of Acts is the only available source that purports to describe the origin of Christianity from the time of Jesus to the arrival in Rome of the great apostle Paul. It is a masterful work in many respects, but controversy continues to swirl over the question of its historical reliability — an issue severely complicated by the paucity of comparative sources.

The book opens with a reference to a "first book" (Acts 1:1), indicating that Acts is a sequel. All readers today agree that the first book was the Gospel of Luke. The two books have the same lucid style and exhibit the similar thematic tendencies. Moreover, the first ends and the second begins with a reference to Jesus' "ascension" (Luke 24:44-52; Acts 1:1-11). Both books are dedicated to a certain Theophilus (Luke 1:3; Acts 1:1), who, because the name means in Greek "friend of God," might be symbolic.

The authorship and date of Acts are unknown. Although the book ends with Paul in Rome awaiting trial, it does not reveal the outcome of the trial nor mention the death of Paul. Scholars today nonetheless agree that the book was written after the death of Paul, perhaps between 80 and 100 C.E. Although both Luke and Acts nowhere mention the name of the author, early Christian tradition is unanimous in attributing both books to one of Paul's traveling companions, Luke the physician (Col. 4:14; Phlm. 24; 2 Tim. 4:11). If this is true, then these, the New Testament's two longest books, are perhaps the only ones in the New Testament not written by Jews. The author tells us that he was not an eyewitness of Jesus' ministry (Luke 1:1-4).

The author uses several literary techniques. He includes summary statements (like a slide in a movie) in the course of the narrative (for example, Acts 2:43-47; 4:32-35). To maintain the readers' interest, he provides a miracle story or human-interest incident at intervals in the narrative (for example, 1:18; 3:1-10; 5:1-16; 9:36-41; 13:6-12; 14:8-10; 19:11-20; 20:9-12). He has the main characters give speeches, sometimes lengthy ones (2:14-36; 3:12-26; 7:2-53; 13:16-41; 20:18-35; 22:2-21; 24:10-21; 26:1-23). And he charts the geographic spread of the new faith from its origin in Jerusalem (chs. 1–7) to Samaria (8:1-39), the seacoast (8:40–9:9), Damascus (9:10–11:18), Antioch and Cyprus (11:19–13:12), Asia Minor (13:13), Europe (16:11), and to the capital, Rome (28:16).

The book centers on two persons, Peter, who represents the Jerusalem church (chs. 2–15), and Paul, "apostle to the Gentiles" (chs. 9–28).

The first section gives an account of the incidents that led to the new believers moving beyond the borders of Judaism to include Gentiles. Among these incidents are:

1. The growth of the original Jerusalem community and the unity among them. Luke narrates that, on the day of Pentecost (a Jewish festival, seven weeks after Passover — or Easter), the Spirit descended on the followers of Jesus in Jerusalem, enabling them to speak the numerous languages of Jewish pilgrims attending the festival from various parts of the world (Acts 2:5, 8-11). After a passionate address by Peter (2:14-39), 3000 persons joined the group. The first summary statement in Acts describes the ideal unity of the group (2:43-47).

2. Tensions among the Jerusalem believers, however, are apparent already in chapter 6, which mentions a dispute between "Hellenists" and "Hebrews," that is, Greek-speaking followers of Jesus and Palestinian, Aramaic-speaking ones. The leader of the first group, Stephen, came to be accused by Jewish leaders of speaking against the temple and the Law of Moses (similar to the charges against Jesus, according to the Gospels). Stephen's defense, the longest speech in Acts (7:2-53), enraged the hearers, who stoned him to death, thus making him the first martyr of the new faith.

3. The death of Stephen drove some believers out of Jerusalem, which led to missionary activity in Samaria (Acts 8:1) and eventually in Phoenicia, Cyprus, and Antioch; but still up to this point "they spoke the word to no one except Jews" (11:19).

4. Acts 10 gingerly narrates one of the decisive moments in the history of Christianity, the conversion of the first Gentile, the Roman centurion Cornelius, "a devout man who feared God with all his household" (10:2), "well spoken of by the whole Jewish nation" (10:22). The church was now a mixed group, which occasioned heated discussion about the admission into the group of uncircumcised Gentiles. Would the followers of Jesus constitute a new religion?

5. Acts attributes the resolution of the issue to a meeting of church leaders — including James, Peter, and Paul — in Jerusalem (ch. 15).

After considerable discussion, the decision was made not to require circumcision of Gentile converts, thus throwing open the door to large-scale conversions of Greeks, Romans, and others (15:19-21).

The second section of Acts describes the energy of the missionary Paul in increasing the numbers of Gentile converts throughout the eastern part of the Mediterranean world, activity that brought quantum changes to the theology and life of the new faith. The reader of Acts has the rare opportunity of comparing the account in chapters 9–28 with Paul's own letters. Among the details found only in Acts — not mentioned in the letters — are Paul's hometown, Tarsus (Acts 9:11, 30; 11:25; 21:39; 22:3), his Roman citizenship (16:37-38; 22:25-29; 23:27), his study in Jerusalem with the great Jewish teacher Gamaliel (22:3; but Paul himself takes pride in his background as a Pharisee; see Phil. 3:5-6), his trade, tentmaking (18:3), and his Hebrew name, Saul (see 13:9). In addition, Paul's speeches in Acts demonstrate a quite different understanding of the new faith compared with his letters. All of this raises the question of the relation between historical information and literary artifice in the book of Acts. The picture of Paul in Acts, however, is strikingly and artfully done.

Paul's coming to faith in Jesus is narrated three times (Acts 9; 22; 26) as occurring near Damascus, to where Paul, as a persecutor of followers of Jesus, was going to seek out believers. According to Acts and Paul's own statements (Gal. 1:14-17; 1 Cor. 9:1; 15:8), the risen Jesus appeared to him and commissioned him to be "apostle to the Gentiles." This revelation forced Paul to a radical switch of loyalties — from persecution of the Jesus movement out of zeal for the Torah to fierce and untiring evangelism for the gospel.

Acts structures Paul's travels into three missionary journeys and a final journey to Rome. The first journey (Acts 13:1–14:28) took him to Cyprus and then to what is now the south-central part of Turkey. His pattern when reaching a town was to seek out the synagogue and there appeal mainly to the adherents of Gentile background, arguing for the resurrection of Jesus and his messiahship. The second journey (15:36–18:22) took him through the places of the first journey and then (16:9) to Europe (Philippi in Greece) and on to Athens and Corinth. On the third journey (18:23–21:17) Paul visited most of the churches he had founded on the first two and — most probably — wrote his greatest surviving letters. He returned by sea from Miletus in Asia Minor to Jerusalem with a collection of money from his Gentile converts to aid the church in Jerusalem, which was suffering from famine and poverty at the time. On his arrival in Jerusalem, Paul was arrested, brought to a Jewish council (22:30), taken to the Roman governor at Caesarea, Felix (23:23-24), and, after two years' delay, brought before Felix's successor, Festus (24:27). On the basis of his Roman citizenship (23:27), Paul insisted that his case be tried in Rome (25:9-12), and Festus concurred. Paul's final journey in Acts (ch. 27) is a vivid account of sea travel in antiquity. Paul arrived in Rome (28:16) and was kept under house arrest, yet free to preach (28:16, 30-31).

Reading Historical and Quasi-Historical Writings

Strange as it might seem, the reading and interpreting of historical sources from antiquity is perhaps more difficult than for most other kinds of literature. The reader must have in mind at least a tentative outline of the course of events described — and this can be derived only from the available sources. More difficult is to determine the gap between the events narrated and the time of writing: to what degree does the source reflect the author's time rather than the time purportedly described? Are there anachronisms and invented events or speeches? Complicating the matter is the fact that the sources frequently use older material, with the result that several "times of writing" are involved. What can the reader do?

A first step is the attempt to determine more precisely the kind of literature. Is it a war song, a tribal legend, royal annals, editorial interpretation, a memoir, a letter, an etiology, a biography, or something else? Although royal annals (like the major source used to narrate the story of the throne succession at the time of King David) often provide good and reliable information, historical writing as a self-conscious genre is generally not found before the Greek Herodotus (5th century B.C.E.), and its closest exemplar in the Bible is perhaps the New Testament book of Acts.

The reader also can observe doublets and triplets, which are numerous in the Bible. For example, there are two accounts of creation (Gen. 1–2), three explanations of the meaning of the name Isaac (Gen. 17:17-19; 18:12-15; 21:6), two stories of the provision of manna and quails during the Israelites' wilderness wanderings (Exod. 16–17; Num. 11), two occurrences of the Ten Commandments (Exod. 20; Deut. 5), three versions of the edict of Cyrus (Ezra 1:2-4; 6:3-5; 2 Chr. 36:22-23), two forms of the "Lord's Prayer" (Matt. 6:9-13; Luke 11:2-4) and of numerous other materials in the Gospels, and three accounts of Paul's vision of the risen Jesus (Acts 9; 22; 26) — to list just a few. Do the parallel texts reveal literary borrowing, common oral tradition, or something else? Can a sequence of development of the text be accomplished?

In some cases repetition indicates the folklorist character of a text. Consider the repetition of conversation in 2 Kgs. 2:1-8: "'Stay here; for YHWH has sent me as far as Bethel [or Jericho or the Jordan].' But Elisha said, 'As YHWH lives, and as you yourself live, I will not leave you.' So they went down to ———. The company of prophets who were in ——— came out to Elisha, and said to him, 'Do you know that today YHWH will take your master away from you?' And he said, 'Yes, I know; keep silent.'" Repetition is especially characteristic of the stories in Daniel 2–7. Mention of "the horn, pipe, lyre, trigon, harp, drum, and entire musical ensemble" and "peoples, nations, and languages" occurs numerous times in chapter 3. Such repetition is typical of oral folklore.

More subtle and yet of great importance is the effort to determine the thematic or ideological tendencies of the text and its author or authors. Entire contingents of biblical scholars now engage in "rhetorical criticism" and "narrative criticism" to describe the slant and themes of narratives. Where does the bias lie in the story of the power struggle between Saul and David in 1 Samuel? Is the picture of the Canaanite religion in the books of Judges and 2 Kings fair? Does a male bias permeate all the narratives? Does the book of Acts minimize the conflict in the early church between those who wanted to remain within Judaism and those who evangelized uncircumcised Gentiles? Do the letters of Paul offer an accurate picture of the Judaism (or Judaisms) of his time?

Such questions involve the more basic issue of the nature of history itself as an object of human inquiry. Why are you interested in ancient documents? Do you seek a paradigm for your own thought and life? Or are you an antiquarian? What does it mean to "understand" the past?

Despite such perplexing questions, many persons will agree that reading brings its own rewards. The engagement between text and reader is a subtle one and often results in widely divergent outcomes.

5

Justice, Judgment, and the Fate of Nations: Prophetic Literature

Many readers have mistakenly assumed that the great prophets of the Old Testament were chiefly concerned with predicting the sweep of future history, the life and work of Jesus, or the end of the world. The tendency to read prophetic oracles as applying directly to our own group can be seen already in the Dead Sea Scrolls, whose writers applied texts from Isaiah, Habakkuk, and other prophetic books to the history of their sect or to the coming of the End in a great war. Such thinking persists today in the Western world, especially among "evangelical" Christians and other groups. I will show in Chapter 7 that such concerns were much more typical of apocalyptic writers than of the classical prophets and that a distinction between prophecy and apocalyptic is essential to an understanding of what the Old Testament prophets were about.

All the great biblical prophets were convinced that they had received words and messages from YHWH to speak to their own people. "Thus says the LORD: . . ." (or, more literally, "Oracle of YHWH: . . .") is a common introduction to a prophet's message. The message was an analysis of the goings-on in the prophet's own time — what had gone wrong, what would happen as a consequence, and what, if anything, could be done to avert disaster.

The *form* of the prophetic word could be oracles (poetic lines in which the first person pronoun denotes YHWH, introduced by "Thus says the LORD"), lyric poetry, visual signs, visions, sermons, prose advice, symbolic actions, and others, depending only on the creativity of the prophet.

The *content* of the message, adapted to the issues of the time, often came as a protest against the prevailing mood of the people. To a people glutted with self-satisfaction or overconfidence the prophet spoke words of judgment and disaster. In times of despair the message was one of comfort and the assurance of a hopeful future. Components of the prophet's message included the ethical (what was right, fair, and just), the social (corrupt institutions, concern for the poor and marginalized), the political (the state might be headed in the wrong direction), and what we could call religious (protest against neighboring cults or reliance on the national cult with its priesthood and sacrificial system, without justice). The prophets, in short, pointed to sin in the lives of the people and in the nation, especially sin that affected the helpless.

Although the idea that God or the gods communicate verbally or visually through humans was widespread in antiquity, the rise of prophecy in Israel cannot be precisely reconstructed. The prophets mentioned in 1 Sam. 10:5-7; 19:19-24 — the period of the first king, Saul — engaged in ecstatic and charismatic activity but probably did not address the historical issues of the time. Some prophets functioned as religious advisers to the kings, paid or unpaid (Samuel to Saul, Nathan to David, Ahijah at the death of Solomon, Micaiah to Ahab, Isaiah to Ahaz and others, Huldah to Josiah, and so on), while others, like Amos and Jeremiah, functioned without external support while making strong statements about the policies of the king.

One of the greatest of prophets in the early part of the Israelite monarchy was Elijah, whose activities are described in a mixture of materials in 1 Kings 17–2 Kings 2. He issued ethical protest against the king's takeover of Naboth's vineyard (1 Kgs. 21). In a time of the ascendancy of Canaanite (= Phoenician) religion in Israel (due to the efforts of Ahab's Phoenician wife, Jezebel), Elijah stimulated a revival of YHWHism at the contest on Mount Carmel (1 Kgs. 18). The political aspect of his work is seen not only in his direct dealings with the king of

Israel but also in his involvement in the throne succession both in Israel and in Syria (1 Kgs. 19). Partly because of the legend of his translation to heaven in a chariot of fire (2 Kgs. 2:9-12), Elijah became the subject of a mass of later traditions, including the belief that he would return to herald the coming of the end of the age or of the Messiah (Mal. 4:5; Mark 6:15; Matt. 11:14; John 1:21).

The *prophetic books* of the Old Testament include three lengthy ones (Isaiah, Jeremiah, and Ezekiel) and "the Book of the Twelve" or the "minor prophets" (Hosea through Malachi). I take as illustrative of the distinctive aspects of prophetic literature, in their historical order, Amos, "First Isaiah" (Isa. 1–39), Jeremiah, and "Second Isaiah" (Isa. 40–55).

Amos of Tekoa (Active about 750 B.C.E.)

The first of the prophets whose message was collected in a book bearing his name, Amos exemplifies the hallmarks of the classical Hebrew prophet. During his time, the two Israelite kingdoms, Judah in the south and Israel in the north, were increasingly threatened by the rise of the Assyrian Empire to the east, in upper Mesopotamia. A shepherd and "a dresser of sycamore trees" from the village of Tekoa, near Bethlehem in Judah (Amos 1:1; 7:10-15), Amos went to Bethel, one of two religious centers in the northern kingdom, Israel, to proclaim judgment ("the day of YHWH") for the lack of justice and for religious apostasy there. Israel had enjoyed relative peace and prosperity during the 40-year reign of its last great king, Jeroboam II (ruled 786-746 B.C.E.), but Amos saw disaster looming. In a series of gripping images and poetic lines, Amos castigated religious hypocrisy and — especially — social injustice in Israel, the punishment for which would be military invasion by Assyria and doom for the nation.

> Seek the LORD and live,
>> or he will break out against the house of Joseph like fire,
>> and it will devour Bethel, with no one to quench it.

Ah, you that turn justice to wormwood,
and bring righteousness to the ground! (Amos 5:6-7)

Take away from me the noise of your songs;
I will not listen to the melody of your harps.
But let justice roll down like waters,
and righteousness like an everflowing stream. (Amos 5:23-24)

Although the central section of the book (Amos 3–6) is a collection of separate oracles and other short judgment poems, chapters 1–2 are a more unified collection of judgments against the nations around Israel, with the prophet zeroing in ever more closely to his audience. Similarly, chapters 7–9 offer a set of five visions of judgment that Amos "saw" (see 1:1): locusts, a supernatural fire, a plumb line, a basket of summer fruit (a Hebrew pun), and a horrifying vision of YHWH destroying the worshipers in the temple.

Amos is a textbook example of a prophet of doom. In his view, religious and moral corruption had reached such a point that the end of the nation could not be averted. He was obsessed with images of fire and military atrocities — but also with the justice of God.

Isaiah of Jerusalem

The more than 50 years of activity of the prophet Isaiah (approximately 742 to 687 B.C.E.) spanned the reigns of four kings in Jerusalem. With the increasing westward expansion of the Assyrian Empire, the mood was one of impending catastrophe. Judah's sister kingdom, Israel, fell to Assyria in 722, and by 701 Assyrian troops were besieging Jerusalem. Throughout this period, Isaiah warned that Assyria should not be resisted; an anti-Assyrian alliance would be a "covenant with death" (Isa. 28:14-18), because Assyria was actually being used by YHWH as a means of judgment ("Assyria, the rod of my anger . . . ," 10:5).

The form of Isaiah's message, called "the vision . . . which he saw" (1:1) or "the word that [he] . . . saw" (2:1), is typically the oracle, in which the prophet speaks the words of YHWH in the first person ("What to me is the multitude of your sacrifices? says the LORD," 1:11). But we find also lyric poems of great power, for example, "swords into plowshares" (2:2-4) and the "Song of the Vineyard" (5:1-7), and a majestic account of the prophet's call vision in the Jerusalem temple (ch. 6).

One passage in Isaiah especially illustrates the importance of recognizing the nature of prophetic literature: the "Sign of Immanuel" in chapter 7. Isaiah 7–8 refers to events of 733-732 B.C.E. Israel and Syria — Judah's neighbors to the north — had formed an alliance to face the threat from the powerful Assyrian Empire and were trying to force Judah to join the coalition. Judah's king, Ahaz, was uncertain what to do. "The heart of Ahaz and the heart of his people shook as the trees of the forest shake before the wind" (7:2). Worried about a siege, the king went to inspect the water supply. There the prophet confronted the king. Isaiah's message was simple: "Take heed, be quiet, do not fear" (7:4). The king was not calmed. Isaiah therefore came to the king again with a "sign": a child would soon be born, presumably to the king and his wife, whose name would be Immanuel ("God with us"): "Look, the young woman is with child and shall bear a son, and shall name him Immanuel" (7:14). Before this child is old enough to distinguish between right and wrong, Assyria would neutralize the threat to Judah from her small neighbors. The prophet's message centered on the name and age of the child and was entirely clear and meaningful to King Ahaz in 732 B.C.E.

The Gospel of Matthew, however, quotes a part of this message in an entirely different way. The Greek translation used by Matthew translated the Hebrew word *almah* ("young woman," married or unmarried) with the Greek word *parthenos* ("virgin"), so that the text reads, "A virgin shall conceive . . ." (Matt. 1:23). For the Gospel writer, the "Sign of Immanuel," therefore, refers to (1) the unique virginal conception of Jesus in his mother's womb and (2) the name Immanuel, signifying God's presence with us in the person of Jesus.

The prophets brought the "word of the LORD" to interpret the events of their own day. Matthew's reading of Isa. 7:14 would have made no sense to King Ahaz. However we read the two texts, it is clear that the threat to Judah from Syria and Israel was the historical context

of Isaiah's message in chapter 7. By the same token, Matthew's reading was typical of interpretive methods used by other Jews and Christians of antiquity.

Among other classic passages in Isaiah are two poems that look forward to the ideal Davidic king in Jerusalem, 9:2-7 and 11:1-9 (both are part of the libretto in Handel's *Messiah*). The image of the Davidic king who would defeat Judah's enemies and inaugurate a universal kingdom of peace and justice anticipates the concept of the Davidic Messiah that was developed over the next centuries in Jewish literature.

Jeremiah and the Fall of Jerusalem

Jeremiah, one of the most gifted of poets in world history, is known to us more directly and intimately than any other Old Testament figure, thanks to the remarkable book that bears his name. A master of lyric judgment poetry, the prophet allows us a first-hand glimpse into his inner torment that accompanied the greatest catastrophe of biblical history — the end of his nation, its monarchy, and its temple at the hands of the Babylonian army.

Jeremiah's prophetic career began in 627 B.C.E. (the 13th year of King Josiah's reign, 1:1-2) and lasted until a few years after the fall of Jerusalem in 587 — a period of more than 40 years. During this time the Assyrian Empire fell and the Babylonian Empire took its place as a threat to the existence of the small states in the Near East. Faced with world-historical upheavals, the kings in Jerusalem had to determine whether to tilt toward Egypt to the west or Babylon — the destroyer of the aggressive Assyrian Empire — to the east. Obsessed with the idea that God would punish Judah for religious and moral depravity, Jeremiah consistently warned of the threat to his nation from "the foe from the north," which by 600 came to be seen as Babylon. Preaching judgment and destruction for several decades at a time when no disaster seemed to happen, Jeremiah became increasingly isolated — from his enemies in the court and at the temple, from his former friends, from his family, and — so he felt — from God. One result is the remarkable

collection of materials in the book of Jeremiah, from first-rate historical information to the first true autobiographical writing in antiquity.

THE BOOK

At least five stages in the compilation of the book of Jeremiah can be identified:

1. In 605 B.C.E. Jeremiah produced a written account of his messages of judgment against Judah (see Jer. 36:1-4), some of which can be seen in the opening chapters of the book (within 1:4–8:3). This includes oracles, lyric poetry, and prose sermonic material — all undated. The king destroyed this first scroll, but Jeremiah rewrote it with additions (Jer. 36:9-32), parts of which might be found in 8:4–10:16, along with possible later additions in 11:1–24:10. Chapters 1–25 thus contain material dating from 626 to 605 and, because its core originated from the prophet himself, can be called "The Jeremiah Book."

2. After Jeremiah's death his disciple, Baruch, wanting to vindicate the prophet and his message, wrote his own account of the momentous events. Baruch often included dates (the year of the king in power). He began with the account of Jeremiah's "Temple Sermon" of 609 B.C.E., in which the prophet predicted the destruction of the Jerusalem temple, and continued to describe the prophet's activities during the siege and fall of Jerusalem and the aftermath, with Jeremiah and Baruch fleeing with others to refuge in Egypt. This biographical material, found in Jeremiah 26–29, 34–45, can be called "The Baruch Book."

3. Chapters 30–33, a collection of messages and symbolic actions of hope, "The Book of Consolation," have an uncertain origin, although several pieces certainly contain accurate historical information.

4. Oracles against neighboring nations are collected in chapters 46–51, much of it originating from a time later than that of Jeremiah.

5. Chapter 52 is a historical summary to the whole anthology, probably contributed by the compiler of the book.

THE MESSAGE OF JUDGMENT

A graphic arrangement of Jeremiah's message of judgment, which led to his ostracism, is found in chapters 2–7. There will be military invasion from the north (4:5-6), leading to the utter destruction of Jerusalem (4:16, 30-31). The land would return to the chaos of pre-creation, waste and void (4:23-26). This horrifying disaster is YHWH's punishment for religious apostasy (ch. 2) and the moral corruption of the people (chs. 5–6). The prophet wonders whether it is too late to repent (ch. 3).

There are two separate accounts, chapters 7 and 26, of a dramatic event in Jeremiah's life. In 609 B.C.E. Jeremiah stood at the gate of the temple in Jerusalem, castigated the people for moral and religious depravity, and predicted the destruction of the temple. Priests and cult prophets demanded the death penalty, but Jeremiah was saved by a prince, Ahikam son of Shaphan (26:24). No longer, however, was he allowed to enter the temple precincts.

Jeremiah called for inward renewal of human life. No external forms would suffice. Consistent with his powers of introspection (but at odds with his priestly ancestry — see 1:1), he spoke of the uselessness of sacrifices and referred to the circumcision of the heart (4:4). While Isaiah had proclaimed that YHWH would intervene *on behalf of* the nation, Jeremiah announced that YHWH would intervene *against* it.

The isolation and torment that this message caused for the prophet are graphically expressed in a series of poems that might be the first truly autobiographical material in history. Included among these "Confessions" are 4:19-22; 8:18-22; 11:18–12:6; 15:10-21; 17:14-18; 18:18-23; and 20:7-18. Jeremiah reveals a compulsion to speak ("a burning fire shut up in my bones," 20:9), even though speaking produces writhing agony and increasing hostility from others. The low point comes when he wonders whether YHWH has given him a false message, a prediction that would not be fulfilled (15:18, "a deceitful

brook"). At some point, however, the prophet's confidence returned and self-doubt vanished (15:19-21).

JEREMIAH'S HOPE

Jeremiah's commission included the command both "to destroy" and also "to build and to plant" (1:10). The "Book of Consolation" is almost evenly divided between poetry (chs. 30–31) and prose (chs. 32–33). Proof that the prophet gave messages of hope even while the city was besieged is the narrative of his purchase of land from his cousin in his hometown, Anathoth, just northeast of Jerusalem. The date and historicity of much of the poetic material are impossible to determine (this includes the return of the northern tribes and the restoration of the Davidic monarchy), but the oracle about the "new covenant" is a classic passage that conveys Jeremiah's long-standing call for inner integrity and spirituality: "I will put my law within them, and will write it on their hearts . . . ; I will forgive their iniquity, and remember their sin no more" (31:31-34).

Second Isaiah and
the Hope for Reconstruction

Scholars today generally agree that Isaiah 40–55, "Second Isaiah," dates from approximately 538 B.C.E. These chapters, which never mention the name Isaiah, presuppose that Judah and Jerusalem are in ruins and predict that they shall be rebuilt. Most striking, a new world-ruler is mentioned by name, Cyrus of Persia (Isa. 44:28; 45:1), and he is called YHWH's "anointed." (This situation is not predicted, but assumed to exist at the time the prophet writes.) Moreover, the distinctive and majestic vocabulary, poetic structure, rhetoric, and meter of Second Isaiah and their difference from the judgment poetry of Isaiah 1–39 can be seen even in English translation.

The main themes of Second Isaiah are clear and powerful:

1. The Judeans (Jews) will return to Jerusalem from Babylonian exile. From beginning to end, Second Isaiah is a joyous proclamation of good news: "Comfort, O comfort my people, says your God" (Isa. 40:1). Cyrus of Persia has defeated (or will shortly defeat) Babylon and permitted the exiles there to return to their respective homelands (see the decree of Cyrus in Ezra 1:2-4; 6:3-5). The prophet takes this decree as an incontrovertible sign that God had forgiven the people; God would renew the covenant with them, and they would be the instrument of salvation for all nations. Like a shepherd, God will "feed his flock" and "gather the lambs in his arms" (40:11).

2. The oneness of God, the clearest expression of monotheism in the Old Testament, is a special emphasis of Second Isaiah. YHWH is the creator of all that is (40:28; 42:5-6; 45:18; and elsewhere) and the sovereign of all nations of the earth, which are "like a drop from a bucket" (40:15-17). This emphasis on the oneness of God leads the prophet not to warn against but to mock idol worship; the classic passage is Isa. 44:9-20.

3. Second Isaiah includes four poems (42:1-4; 49:1-6; 50:4-9; 52:13–53:12) that describe an enigmatic "servant" whose task it is to "bring Jacob back to YHWH" (that is, to bring the dispersed people back to Judah) and to be "a light to the nations, that my [YHWH's] salvation may reach to the end of the earth" (49:5-6). The fourth Servant Song (52:13–53:12) asserts that the servant had a repugnant appearance and was "despised and rejected by others; a man of suffering and acquainted with infirmity; and as one from whom others hide their faces he was despised, and we held him of no account" (53:3). Those who had known the servant, however, became convinced that the humiliation and suffering of this figure were "for our transgressions"; "surely he has borne our infirmities and carried our diseases" (53:4-5). The servant was not being punished for wrongdoing on his part but was suffering vicariously. His humiliation continued even to his ignominious burial (53:9). Because of the servant's willingness to take on a divine mission, God will ultimately exalt him and allot him "a portion with the great" (53:12).

What is the function of the Servant Songs within Second Isaiah? Is (or was) the servant an individual or simply a collective idea? Was his work to take place in the prophet's time or in the future? Supporters of the collective interpretation point to 49:3, "You are my servant, Israel, in whom I will be glorified." The details in the fourth poem, however, are descriptive of an individual. Although the interpretations of these songs are as numerous and diverse as their readers, we might think that the poems originally told the story of a man — perhaps a leper — who was known by the poet, a man whose suffering and isolation were great. The genius of the original poems was to convey the idea of vicarious suffering — some persons do suffer more than they deserve, but this suffering can have redemptive and truth-bringing potential. Second Isaiah then took up the poems as a symbol of Judah's history and task. Judah had suffered in the exile more than she deserved, and her task now is to be "a light to the nations," that is, to bring the knowledge of the one God to all the peoples of the earth.

Christians have traditionally found parallels to the life, death, and resurrection of Jesus in Isaiah 53 (much of the text is used in Handel's *Messiah*). There are express quotations of the passage in the New Testament — but fewer than we might expect. Although there are general parallels between the servant and the life and fate of Jesus, there is no reason to think that the allusions to the physical condition of the servant were descriptive of Jesus. On matters of this sort, a distinction between parallels and predictions must be observed in order to respect the integrity of the original context of the writings. Moreover, the servant and the Messiah are two different figures. According to Jewish tradition, the messianic function is accomplished by military victories and the establishment of a universal kingdom of peace and justice headquartered in Jerusalem — ideas foreign to the Servant Songs.

Recognizing and Reading
Prophetic Literature

Prophetic literature apart from the prophetic books is sparse. Messages expressly attributed to prophets are found scattered in the books of

Samuel (for example, 1 Sam. 15:22-23; 2 Sam. 12:1-15) and Kings (for example, 1 Kgs. 11:29-39; within the Elijah/Elisha stories in 1 Kgs. 17–2 Kgs. 13; and 2 Kgs. 22:14-20). Although scholars debate the origin of specific texts in the prophetic books, the content of these books as a whole constitutes a describable literary form.

In the prophetic literature it is helpful to distinguish oracles (poems in which the first person pronouns — I, me, mine — refer to YHWH) from other poetic types. Oracles, the distinctive, perhaps unique form of prophetic expression, immediately reveal the prophets' self-understanding: they spoke the words of God to interpret the great historical and international events of their time. They therefore functioned as social, political, and religious commentators.

Because of this basic function, even a general understanding of a specific prophetic message requires at least minimal knowledge of the events that the prophet was interpreting. Without this, the prophets' messages will certainly be wrenched out of context and read in a way that the original speaker would find completely unintelligible. This misapplication of prophetic texts is well documented already in the Dead Sea Scrolls and in the traditional Christian tendency to read the prophets as predictors of the coming of Jesus.

To gain a sense of the prophets' interpretation of major events and conditions of their time, read the account of the end of the Northern Kingdom, Israel, in 2 Kgs.14:23–17:41. Then, in one sitting, read the book of Amos and imagine how his words would have been heard by citizens experiencing a time of strength and prosperity before the final end. Note the alternation of oracles, other poetry, and visual symbols in this book.

Similarly, read the account of the end of the Southern Kingdom, Judah, in 2 Kings 22–25 and then observe Jeremiah's message in Jer. 1–7; 31:31-34; 32:1-15. Again, observe the prophet's use of oracles, lyric poetry, sermons, and symbolic actions to convey his understanding of the will of God in a specific and dire situation.

6

Regulating Life: Legal Collections

Regulation of life in social groups is universal and timeless among humans. Among the oldest human literary remains are legal materials, for example, the laws of Hammurabi of Babylon (18th century B.C.E.). The Old Testament contains several ancient Israelite collections of laws, precepts, and other regulations, the chief of which are found in the books of Exodus, Leviticus, Numbers, and Deuteronomy. Development of church regulations among the early Christians is also evidenced from an early period, as the Gospel of Matthew and the Pastoral Epistles indicate.

Old Testament Collections

THE TEN COMMANDMENTS

The Ten Commandments (see Exod. 34:28; Hebrew: "Ten Words") or Decalogue, which appear in Exod. 20:1-17 and Deut. 5:6-21 (see also Exod. 34:11-26), have exercised an influence on Western civilization that can scarcely be exaggerated. They are presented in Exodus 20 as direct address of God to the people at the time of Moses and the exodus, but neither the date of the present form of the text nor the authorship can be determined.

66

In the classic form, Exod. 20:1-17, the commandments are prefaced by reference to the deliverance from Egypt: "I am YHWH your God, who brought you out of the land of Egypt, out of the house of slavery" (v. 2). It is thereby clear that the commandments are rooted in the idea of the covenant relationship between YHWH and Israel and are considered the proper response of the people for YHWH's saving activity on their behalf.

Reference to the commandments being written on two stone "tablets" or "tables" (Exod. 24:12; 34:1) has led many readers to distinguish two kinds of commands. The first several commandments refer to the sole worship of YHWH, reverencing the name YHWH, and the keeping of the Sabbath. (Roman Catholics and Lutherans do not number the prohibition of idols among the commandments, and they separate the prohibition of coveting into two, the ninth and the tenth.) The remainder deal with interhuman relationships: honoring parents, and avoiding killing, adultery, theft, false witness, and coveting. All but two of the commandments (regarding the Sabbath and the honoring of parents) are blanket prohibitions: "You shall not . . ."; that is, they are categorical or apodictic laws.

Because of their categorical nature, with no suggestion regarding their possible implementation (for example, how can coveting be judged and penalized?), the Ten Commandments function more as a series of principles than as a law code. How these principles could be applied in concrete cases is suggested in other collections of law in the Old Testament, for example, the Covenant Code.

The Ten Commandments occupy the center of the Torah, the Pentateuch. Each of the commandments harks back to related narratives in the book of Genesis. For example, the commandment regarding the Sabbath relates to the institution of the Sabbath in Gen. 2:2-3, and there are several narratives in Genesis that deal with honoring or dishonoring one's parents, murder, sexual misdeeds, and coveting. Moreover, subsequent law codes, like the entire book of Deuteronomy, can be read as a commentary on the Ten Commandments.

THE COVENANT CODE

Imbedded in the narrative of the making the Mosaic covenant (Exodus 19–24) is an ancient collection of laws of unknown origin known as the "Covenant Code," Exod. 20:22–23:33. Today's readers note the juxtaposition of "moral" and "ritual" laws in this section. Rules about the treatment of strangers and about bribery in Exodus 23 (vv. 8-9) are found side by side with rules about festivals, offerings, and other cultic matters. (A sharp distinction between ritual and moral emerges in the great prophets.) Like the other codes of the Old Testament, the Covenant Code regulated many aspects of life — religious, family, social, and economic.

Exodus 20–23, moreover, contain both categorical (absolute or apodictic) laws and conditional (or case) laws. Among the categorical laws, which are most often blanket prohibitions or requirements with no gradations, are the Ten Commandments and parts of the Covenant Code, such as 22:18-20. Such laws do not distinguish degrees of culpability nor the circumstances, and the penalty, if any is specified, is usually death. Conditional laws are based on the premise of proportionality — the punishment must fit the crime ("an eye for an eye," Exod. 21:24) — and therefore aim at assessing the degree of intentionality behind the crime (see, for example, 21:28-32). Some of the conditional laws, even in the Covenant Code, have parallels with earlier ancient Near Eastern legal collections, like the Code of Hammurabi. All Western law codes are based on the concept of conditional laws.

LAWS IN DEUTERONOMY

Materials in the book of Deuteronomy reflect a long history of traditions, even though the entire book is presented as a speech by Moses to the people of Israel on the plains of Moab just before they crossed the Jordan River to begin the conquest of Canaan.

The core of the book is the law code of Deuteronomy 12–26, the contents of which correspond with the steps taken in King Josiah's religious reform of 622-621 B.C.E., described in 2 Kings 22–23, especially the centralizing of worship and the measures taken to root out vestiges of the polytheism of the neighboring peoples that had invaded Judah. The fact that Deuteronomic influence can be detected not only in the events of those years but also in the editing of Israel's great historical epic, Joshua–2 Kings, indicates the importance of the tradition reflected in this book.

The laws in Deuteronomy have a strongly humanitarian content, with special concern for the poor, the oppressed, the widow, and the orphan. Attention is given also to the natural world, with laws about kindness to animals and care of plants and the land itself. In addition, there are repeated warnings against idolatry and, in chapter 12, laws that center all worship in one place (the temple in Jerusalem is to be understood).

A particularly significant text, a central part of Jewish piety yet today, is Deut. 6:4-9, known by the first Hebrew word in the passage, *Shema*:

> Hear, O Israel, the LORD is our God, the LORD alone. You shall love the LORD your God with all your heart, and with all your soul, and with all your might. Keep these words that I am commanding you today in your heart. Recite them to your children and talk about them when you are at home and when you are away, when you lie down and when you rise. Bind them as a sign on your hand, fix them as an emblem on your forehead, and write them on the doorposts of your house and on your gates.

THE HOLINESS CODE

Leviticus 17–26, because of its emphasis on the holiness of God and people, has come to be known as the "Holiness Code": "You shall be holy to me, for I YHWH am holy . . ." (Lev. 20:26). Included are regulations about sexual conduct (ch. 18), cultic requirements, penalties, priestly instructions, festivals and Sabbaths, the Year of Jubilee (ch. 25), and the teaching of the "two ways" (ch. 26). Among the ritual concerns there occurs one of the loftiest of moral principles: "You shall not take vengeance or bear a grudge against any of your people, but you shall love your neighbor as yourself: I am YHWH" (19:18).

OTHER LEGAL MATERIALS IN THE OLD TESTAMENT

In addition to the Holiness Code, Leviticus contains regulations on sacrifices (chs. 1–7), priests and their office (chs. 8–10), clean and unclean (edible or not) animals (ch. 11), women in childbirth (ch. 12), lepers and bodily discharges (chs. 13–15), the Day of Atonement (Yom Kippur, ch. 16), and vows (ch. 27).

The book of Numbers, mainly priestly in editing, includes laws on the Levites (chs. 4; 8; 18), adultery (ch. 5), vows (chs. 6; 30), sacrifices (ch. 15), uncleanness (ch. 19), inheritance (ch. 27), sacrifices and festivals (chs. 28–29), and cities of refuge (ch. 35).

Laws also occur in narrative contexts, for example, on circumcision in Gen. 17:9-14 and on Passover in Exodus 12.

The Beginnings of
Christian Legal Traditions

As the groups of early Christians spread, the need arose to find means to settle disputes and lapses of various kinds within the communities of believers, not all of which could be arbitrated by appeal to Old Testament laws. (The attitudes of early Christians toward the ongoing authority of the legal codes of the Old Testament ranged widely — from complete acceptance to virtual rejection — but the subject is too complex to deal with in this context.) Such disputes are evidenced in the Gospels, the letters, and Revelation.

Matt. 18:15-22 can be read as an example of the beginnings of Christian disciplinary tradition:

If another member of the church sins against you, go and point out the fault when the two of you are alone. If the member listens to you, you have regained that one. But if you are not listened to, take one or two others along with you, so that every word may be confirmed by the evidence of two or three witnesses. If the member refuses to listen to them, tell it to the church, and if the offender refuses to listen even to the church, let such a one be to you as a Gentile and a tax collector. Truly I tell you, whatever you bind on earth will be bound in heaven, and whatever you loose on earth will be loosed in heaven.

Matthew's church adopted the rule of two or three witnesses from Deut. 19:15 (compare 17:6 and Num. 35:30). The manuscript variants for this text also reveal that some took the passage to refer to any person in the community who had fallen into sin, while others read it as legislation for dealing with someone who has sinned against you. In any case, the threefold process is intended to "regain" the offender, not to punish. A similar procedure was recommended by Paul in 1 Cor. 6:1-6.

It was to be expected that later Christians would take judgments from various parts of the New Testament as authoritative in the settling of disputes. Such judgments govern the selection and behavior of church leaders (1 Tim. 3:1-13) but also — and frequently — almost all aspects of the life of ordinary believers (lists of virtues and vices typically appear toward the end of the New Testament letters, and the epistle of James has little else). Particularly vituperative comments on dissidents — with less helpful suggestions on how to deal with them — are found in Revelation 2–3.

Reading Legal Material in the Bible

Legal traditions offer important information about the social conditions of the time of their origin, but their use in this way is often severely limited by our uncertainty of the date of ancient law codes. We can date the New Testament writings to the latter half of the 1st century and the beginning of the 2nd, but reconstruction of the literary history of Israelite law codes is an incredibly complex endeavor.

The question of the relevance of biblical law to persons and communities today is equally challenging. It is obvious that many such laws are no longer followed in Western society (for example, animal sacrifice is no longer practiced), and the application of biblical and talmudic law to daily life is one of the major factors that distinguish branches of Judaism from each other today. Christians also are divided on the meaning and validity of New Testament statements on homosexuality, women in leadership positions in the church, and divorce — among many other topics.

Readers can rather easily recognize legal materials in the Bible. It is helpful to note whether a specific law or collection of laws deals with human obligations to God ("cultic" laws) or relationships between and among humans ("moral" laws). Note also whether the laws are absolute or conditional. Christian readers especially need to recognize that conditional laws are based on a just and universally accepted legal principle, "an eye for an eye," which means simply that the punishment must not exceed the crime.

7

The Appeal to the Future: Apocalyptic Literature

Although influenced partly by prophetic and wisdom traditions, apocalyptic literature as it emerged after the Babylonian exile is unique in several respects and should not be confused with either of those predecessors. We are dealing here with concepts of "the late great planet Earth," being "left behind," and the wrap-up of history as we know it.

The word "apocalypse" comes from the Greek and means "revelation." What is revealed in an apocalypse are the secrets of the heavenly world or of the end of history — or both. The literature comes from a threatened, persecuted, or dispossessed — albeit literate — group that viewed its times as hopelessly and irredeemably corrupt. Unlike the classical prophets, apocalypticists did not preach repentance — it was too late for that. Instead, they looked for the imminent destruction of the present order and the establishment of a glorious kingdom of peace and justice for the faithful, while the evil powers of the present would receive their comeuppance.

In order to calculate the date of the in-breaking of the new age, the apocalypticist often included surveys of history — past, present, and future — encoded in bizarre symbolism, with succeeding epochs referred to as animals, metals, alternating colors, or symmetrical numbers of years. Because the writer often took the nom de plume of an ancient worthy (Enoch, Abraham, Moses, Elijah, Baruch, or another), the survey of past history is typically presented as a prediction of what is to come, that is, it is backdated. The date of writing, the origin, of an apocalypse can thus be set at that point in the historical survey at which the details become vague or incorrect.

All apocalypses presuppose a strong dualism between this historical epoch and the age to come (whether a messianic age, the kingdom of God, or something else). Balanced with this linear contrast is the dualism between the corrupted cosmos in which we live and the abode of God — a dualism of existence, realms, or realities. In the late period of Old Testament history, God was considered too transcendent and remote to communicate directly with humans. The apocalypticists therefore use the media of dreams, visions, or angels to convey revelation from God. Along with heavenly messengers, Satan becomes God's archenemy. New in apocalypses also is a clear emphasis on life beyond death, including the concept of the resurrection of the body.

Apocalypses, in short, are literature of despair that appeals to a glorious, supernatural future soon to come. Despite the apocalypticists' denunciations of the holders of power at their time, we should not assume that their works reflect the thinking of the underclass. Jewish and Christian apocalypses reflect a developed literary tradition and often include passages of poetic power. Although apocalyptic-like texts can be found already in rather late texts in Isaiah, Ezekiel, and Zechariah, the genre flourished in the period from roughly 200 B.C.E. to 100 C.E. The prime biblical examples are the book of Daniel and the book of Revelation (the Apocalypse), along with parts of Matthew, Mark, Luke, and letters like 2 Thessalonians.

The Book of Daniel

The book of Daniel consists of six stories of a folktale type (chs. 1–6) and four dream-visions (chs. 7–12) in typically apocalyptic style. The date of the book in its present form can be determined by a close look at its veiled historical surveys (found in both halves of the book), with an eye toward the point at which the historical allusions become vague or incorrect. For example, Dan. 11:31 asserts that

> Forces sent by [the contemptible person] shall occupy and profane the temple and fortress. They shall abolish the regular burnt offering and set up the abomination that makes desolate. He shall seduce with intrigue those who violate the covenant; but the people who are loyal to their God shall stand firm and take action.

A comparison of this verse with 1 Macc. 1:54 shows that the author of Daniel was aware of the profanation of the temple in 167 B.C.E. (see above, Chapter 4). Daniel brings the narrative further: Jewish resisters will receive "a little help" (Dan. 11:34), possibly a reference to the Maccabean fighters, but the author counsels patient endurance, not active resistance. The Syrians would set up a pagan cult in the temple (11:36-39). In Dan. 11:39, however, the survey of past history ends and actual predictions for the future begin. The author predicts a second invasion of Egypt by the Syrian king Antiochus and refers to a final battle "between the sea and the beautiful holy mountain" (11:45), that is, between the Mediterranean and Jerusalem. In this battle, Daniel predicts, Antiochus IV "Epiphanes" would be killed. In actuality, Antiochus died in 163 B.C.E. in Persia during an attempt to seize the treasures of another temple. Had the author been aware of the rededication of the Jerusalem temple in 164, he would surely have mentioned it. The book of Daniel in its present form, therefore, can with confidence be dated between the years 167 and 164 B.C.E.

THE SIX STORIES (DANIEL 1–6)

Although the six narratives of Daniel and his friends (chs. 1–6) exhibit several features of traditional children's stories (groups of threes, monotonous repetition of phrases, exaggerated heroism), they were probably written for adults. Their presumptive setting is the royal courts of the Babylonians and the Persians, and many of the details (zookeeping, musical instruments) are known to be accurate for the indicated settings. The story, however, is simply the medium for the message, which is a plea to be faithful during intense persecution.

The sequence of historical epochs in the book of Daniel can be seen in the story of Nebuchadnezzar's dream (ch. 2). Daniel's challenge is not merely to interpret the dream but to remind the king what it was he had dreamed. The king saw a "great statue" composed of different metals: golden head, silver chest and arms, bronze torso and thighs, iron legs, and feet partly of iron and partly of clay (2:31-33). In the dream the king saw a stone cut "not by human hands" strike the statute, shattering it from the feet upwards. Then "the stone that struck the statue became a great mountain and filled the whole earth" (v. 35). Daniel then tells the king that the metals represent a succession of worldly powers (2:36-45):

- Gold: Babylon
- Silver: Media
- Bronze: Persia
- Iron: Alexander's empire

The mixture of iron and clay represents the division of Alexander's Greek empire between the Seleucids of Syria and the Ptolemies of Egypt. The supernaturally cut stone is the kingdom of God, which the author suggests would succeed the Greek kingdoms.

THE FOUR DREAM-VISIONS (DANIEL 7–12)

Through the medium of something half-way between dreams and visions, Daniel sees four beasts succeeded by a "son of man" (ch. 7), a ram and a he-goat (ch. 8), a schema of 70 weeks (ch. 9), and a survey of the last things (chs. 10–12). A succession of kingdoms identical to that of Daniel 2 recurs in Daniel 7: a lion with eagle's wings, a bear, a leopard, a terrible beast with iron teeth and 10 horns, and one "like a human being" (literally, "a son of man"), the last of which symbolizes the "holy ones of the Most High" and the kingdom of God (Dan. 7:25, 27). Daniel 7 is the earliest written narrative of final judgment and the prototype for the form of many later Jewish and Christian apocalyptic writings.

This schema is fleshed out in the following chapters, especially chapter 11. The book ends with a prediction of the coming of the angel Michael and a time of unprecedented "anguish" (12:1). Then the people of God, all of whose names are "written in the book," will be delivered. The dead shall rise from the dust of the earth, "some to everlasting life, and some to shame and everlasting contempt" (12:2). The "wise shall shine like the brightness of the sky," becoming like stars (12:3). This is the clearest — and possibly the only — expression of belief in the resurrection of the dead that can be found in the Old Testament.

The Revelation to John

The New Testament Apocalypse, the Revelation to John, consists of an introduction (Rev. 1:1-20), seven letters to the churches of Asia Minor (chs. 2–3), and predictions of what is to happen "soon" (chs. 4–22; see 1:1).

The body of the book, chapters 4–22, is apocalyptic literature, as the author indicates already in the title he provides: "The revelation [Greek: *apokalypsis*] of Jesus Christ, which God gave to show his servants what must soon take place . . ." (1:1).

The earliest Christian tradition dates the book to the close of the reign of Domitian (d. 96 C.E.), a Roman emperor who instigated a persecution of Christians in parts of the empire. During his lifetime he claimed to be worthy of divine worship and appropriated for himself the title "our Lord and our God." In 96 C.E. members of his own household were charged with "atheism," an accusation often leveled against Christians by virtue of their denying the Greek and Roman gods; some of the emperor's family appear to have been persecuted as Christians during this time. In Rev. 2:10 persecution is expected from the authorities, and all Christendom is threatened (3:10). The author, "John" (1:1), sees the harlot, Babylon/Rome, drunk from the blood of the saints and the witnesses of Jesus. Numerous references to martyrs are sprinkled throughout the book (6:10; 16:6; 18:24; 19:2; and elsewhere).

The book claims to have been written by "John" (1:1, 4, 9; 22:8) — but which John? Although some Christian writers of the late 2nd century believed this was John the apostle, one of the original followers of Jesus, others, on linguistic and stylistic grounds, argued the author was another John, a Jewish-Christian prophet writing from the island of Patmos, off the coast of Asia Minor (1:9). Because of wide differences in language and themes, scholars today generally agree that this writer is not the author of the Gospel of John nor of the letters of John.

Even though the author says at the outset that his revelation centers on "what must soon take place" (1:1), some readers have thought that the book contains predictions of events that would take place hundreds or even thousands of years after he wrote. Others have believed that the book is a symbolic forecast of the course of history from the time of the author to the end of the world; such readers have therefore tried to identify various mythological figures in the book — like the great beast — with historical persons. Others have viewed the book as a Graeco-Roman drama of seven acts, each of which has seven scenes. The book, however, is a standard apocalypse, written for the strengthening of Christians in the Roman province of Asia in about 95 c.e. who were threatened with persecution from Rome.

The main theme of Revelation is similar to that of other apocalypses. There is a death struggle going on between the churches and the pagan political power. The Roman state is the "beast," the bitter enemy of the church (13:1-10), and the city of Rome is the "great whore" who sits on the beast (17:1-6). Rome prepares itself for the assault on Christianity, but what has happened up to that time is only a mild foretaste of the imminent decisive struggle, the "hour of trial that is coming on the whole world" (3:10).

For John, behind this earthly drama is a much vaster plane, the war between God and Satan. The Roman Empire is the Satanic world power, because it demands emperor worship (13:4). "Another beast" (13:11-18), also called the "false prophet" (16:13; 19:20; 20:10), is probably the imperial priesthood of the province.

The outcome of the struggle is the subject of a secret scroll with seven seals (5:1). The scroll shows how the might of the empire is broken by Christ, who conquers and destroys the beast and the false prophet (19:11). Then comes the thousand-year reign of Christ and the risen martyrs. Satan is released for his final madness on earth, but he is then destroyed (20:7-10). Following the last judgment (20:11-15) there is revealed a luminous view of a new, glorious world with a new Jerusalem (21:1–22:5), in which death, mourning, crying, pain, and tears will be no more (21:4).

Revelation is a wrenching cry for justice in an unjust world and can be read as a plea to God to redress the grievances of all who suffer in any age. But it stands as a polar opposite to Paul's statements about Christians being subject to the "authorities that be" (Rom. 13:1-7), and it contains cries for revenge (Rev. 6:10) that are quite unlike the teaching of Jesus in the Sermon on the Mount (Matt. 5–7)

Reading Apocalyptic Literature

The first principle of all biblical interpretation applies with full force when we read apocalyptic literature: the text must have had specific meaning to its first readers. The book of Daniel makes good sense in the context of the Maccabean revolt, as does the book of Revelation when seen in the context of Roman persecution of Christians in Asia Minor at the end of the 1st century C.E. The predictive form of material in apocalypses and their insistence on the nearness of the end raise the question of whether we are dealing with unfulfilled predictions. Understood as literature of despair, cries for justice, and calls for the reversal of power, however, such documents retain their effectiveness in any case and can have a strong impact on readers of all ages.

Readers today can easily identify an apocalypse by its bizarre imagery, its symbolic periodization of history, its warnings of an imminent end, its claim to divine revelation, its consistent themes of world-historical struggle, and its depiction of a glorious, supernatural realm soon to be inaugurated.

8

I Want You to Know: Letters

Letters are frequently attested in the Old Testament and constitute the majority of the books of the New. The identifying marks of a letter are simple and universal: the name of the intended recipient or recipients, a message, and the name of the sender or senders. Letters also may contain opening and closing greetings, thanksgiving, compliments, and references to past associations. Over the centuries of biblical history, a clear distinction emerges between official letters (correspondence with or from rulers or city councils, legal briefs, encyclicals, and such) and the "familiar letter" or "friendly letter," which is a substitute for personal conversation (correspondence between friends, family, colleagues, and the like).

Other distinctions are sometimes made among letters of the New Testament period:

- Epistles and letters: An "epistle" is a writing in letter style that is intended for publication or posterity, while "letter" suggests personal correspondence to the named addressees. Under this distinction, Paul's letters and 2-3 John are personal correspondence, and Hebrews, 1-2 Peter, 1 John, and Jude are epistles. (Among Paul's letters, Romans comes closest to resembling a letter intended for publication.)
- Genuine letters and fictional letters: 2 Thess. 2:2 shows that letters

could be forgeries intended to deceive, but numerous Christian documents from the first two centuries are harmless literary fiction, such as the correspondence between Paul and Seneca and the "Letter to the Laodiceans" (prompted by the reference in Col. 4:16). Fictional or literary letters are obviously quite different from friendly letters, and the occasion that led to their writing is often difficult to determine.

Letters in the Old Testament

The first reference to a letter in the Old Testament is the infamous sealed message from King David to his army leader, Joab, sent by the hand of the soldier Uriah (2 Sam. 11:14-15). The king had committed adultery with Uriah's wife, Bathsheba, and now commanded Joab to put Uriah in the heat of battle so that he would be killed. The core of the letter is quoted in v. 15.

Letters were sent also by Queen Jezebel to the elders of Jezreel in the northern kingdom, Israel (1 Kgs. 21:8-10); the king of Damascus to the king of Israel (2 Kgs. 5:5-6); and Jehu, king of Israel, to Samaria (2 Kgs. 10:1-3). In 2 Kgs. 19:8-14 a message from an Assyrian leader is delivered orally to King Hezekiah of Jerusalem, but the king is said to have "received the letter from the hand of the messengers" (v. 14), indicating that such correspondence was given both orally and in writing.

Ezra 4–6 summarizes several diplomatic letters sent and received between Jewish leaders in Judea and the Persian king during the period of the rebuilding of Judea after the Babylonian exile. The biblical text not only refers to the translation of letters (Ezra 4:7) and the oral reading of them (4:23) but also offers what purports to be the actual wording of their contents (4:11-16; 4:17-22; 5:7-17; 6:6-12), which center on the Persian government's approval of the rebuilding of the temple in Jerusalem.

In the Apocrypha, numerous letters are attested in 1-2 Maccabees, in addition to correspondence between Eleazar, high priest in Jerusalem, and the Ptolemies in Egypt (the "Letter of Aristeas"), and the so-called Letter of Jeremiah.

JEREMIAH'S LETTER TO THE EXILES IN BABYLON

According to Jeremiah 29, in about 594 B.C.E. — a few years after the first Babylonian capture of Jerusalem and the deportation of its leaders to Babylon but before the final destruction of Judah — the prophet Jeremiah sent a letter to the Jewish exiles there, the content of which is given in Jer. 29:4-23. At the close of the chapter, reference is made to a letter of response from the prophet Shemaiah in Babylon intended for the religious leaders in Jerusalem (29:25, 29) and to Jeremiah's subsequent denunciation of Shemaiah (29:30-32).

The main theme and purpose of the letter are expressed in Jer. 29:4-9 — the exiles are to accept their situation in Babylon as the will of Yahweh. They are not to be led astray by optimistic prophets who promise a speedy return to Jerusalem but rather to carry on the ordinary duties of life — to build and plant, engage in family life, and "seek the welfare of the city where I have sent you into exile" (vv. 5-7). Jeremiah amplifies this oracle by predicting that the exile will last 70 years, after which the return can take place. (The exile can be dated either from 598 or from 587 B.C.E.; Cyrus's edict allowing the return was actually issued in about 538.)

Jeremiah's letter is another in a long list of means used by the prophets to communicate their message. It reflects his consistent proclamation of judgment on Judah and Jerusalem as well as his unshakable faith that Yahweh still had a future for the people in their ancestral homeland.

Letters in the New Testament

If a letter is defined as a message with named addressees and a named sender (apart from the titles supplied for documents by later copyists, readers, or scholars), there are in the New Testament 13 letters of Paul, in addition to letters by James, Peter (two), and Jude. Although Hebrews has an epistolary ending, it is an anonymous document without specified addressees. First John has none of the essential marks of a letter, even though references to a specific person and to false teachings appear to reflect a concrete situation in the early church. Second John, directed to "the elect lady and her children" (1:1), and 3 John, "to the beloved Gaius" (1:1), both purport to have been written by "the elder." It is common, therefore, to refer to "the Pauline corpus" of 13 letters and the "general letters" or "catholic letters," those addressed to a wider or less clearly specified readership than Paul's letters.

THE PAULINE CORPUS

Some of Paul's letters are — with little doubt — the earliest Christian writings to have survived from antiquity (the Gospels of the New Testament in their present form are all subsequent to Paul's genuine letters). Quite apart from the inherent interest of their subject matter, therefore, they have a unique importance in the reconstruction of the history of earliest Christianity.

It is nonetheless difficult to date Paul's letters. The order of the letters in our Bibles is based on two principles: (1) the letters to churches precede those to individuals and (2) within these two groups they are arranged from longest to shortest. In assigning approximate dates of writing, we are dependent on occasional personal references in the letters that can be correlated with statements in Acts and — less frequently — with nonbiblical information. In Romans, for example, Paul stated that he was about to return to Jerusalem and that he hoped he would soon thereafter journey to Spain via Rome (Rom. 1:10; 15:23-25). In the book of Acts Paul returns to Jerusalem in chapter 21; Acts relates Paul's trip to Rome in chapter 27 and ends with Paul in the city, suggesting, however, that Paul was put to death there by the emperor (Nero).

Within the Pauline corpus, the earliest letters are most probably 1-2 Thessalonians, approximately 50 C.E., while his core letters, Galatians, Romans, and 1-2 Corinthians, come from the years 54-57. The date of the so-called prison letters (the author purports to write from prison) — Colossians, Philemon, Philippians, and Ephesians — is not known, as is the case also with the "pastoral letters," 1-2 Timothy and Titus. (Many scholars have questioned whether Paul is the actual author of the Pastorals and Ephesians.) All of Paul's letters were written to deal with specific situations. To illustrate, 1 Corinthians is a treatment of several problems among Paul's converts in the church at Corinth, and Romans was written as a letter of introduction in the hope that the Roman church would serve as a base for Paul's missionary activity in Spain.

First Corinthians

This problem-centered letter enables us to see some of the inner life of a mid-1st century Gentile congregation in Greece and also to observe the way Paul dealt with questions of morality and values. Chapters 1–6 are a response to issues communicated to Paul by "Chloe's people" (see 1:11), presumably members of the Corinthian church, while chapters 7–15 respond to "the matters about which you wrote" (7:1). Throughout the letter are references to communications, whether oral or written, between Paul and members of the Corinthian church. The list of problems constitutes the outline of the letter:

1. Party-strife within the congregation (chs. 1–4). Chloe's people had reported to Paul that there were four competing groups in the church at Corinth (akin to the game of "favorite pastor"), centered on Paul, Apollos, Peter (here called by his Aramaic name, Cephas), and Christ. The way Paul writes these first four chapters indicates that the major tension in Corinth was between the partisans of Paul and those of Apollos, a Christian teacher from Alexandria in Egypt (see Acts 18:24–19:7), who was a skilled orator and adept at presenting the Christian message in an intellectual and rational framework. Paul in response insists on the "foolishness" of the Christian message which, according to him, centers on the crucified Messiah, something that appeared ludicrous to Jews, who expected a warrior Messiah, and to Greeks, who would wonder how someone executed as a criminal could be the object of worship:

   For Jews demand signs and Greeks desire wisdom, but we proclaim Christ crucified, a stumbling block to Jews and foolishness to Gentiles, but to those who are the called, both Jews and Greeks, Christ the power of God and the wisdom of God. (1 Cor. 1:22-24)

Moreover, he insists that there can be only one foundation of the church, namely, Christ (3:11).

2. Sexual immorality (chs. 5–6). Paul abruptly turns to a case of incest: "It is actually reported that there is sexual immorality among you, and of a kind that is not found even among pagans; for a man is living with his father's wife" (5:1). Because Paul does not label this as a case of adultery, it is probable that a man had married his stepmother, which was forbidden both in Roman and in Jewish law. He advises that the Corinthians cannot tolerate this situation. Beyond that, however, his command that the church members "hand this man over to Satan for the destruction of the flesh" (5:5) is puzzling to us — even if the meaning was clear to the 1st-century Corinthians (perhaps these words refer to excommunication). In response to the Corinthian idea that sexual activity has as little to do with spirituality as does eating, Paul refers to the human body as a "temple of the Holy Spirit" (6:19).

3. Marriage and divorce (ch. 7). Paul now turns to questions put to him in a letter from Corinth. The first is whether Christians should continue to marry if the end is near (this is the probable meaning of "the impending crisis" in 7:26). Paul's response has caused extended comment over the centuries: Indeed, the end is near, and the primary purpose of marriage — procreation — is therefore no longer relevant. The Corinthians should not change their marital status, for "the present form of this world is passing away" (7:31). Marriage nonetheless is the proper arrangement for the release of sexual energy (7:9, 36), even though Paul himself prefers celibacy and wishes that all were as he is (7:7; the argument that Paul was married or a widower has little or no basis in the texts).

4. Food offered to idols (chs. 8–10). Here and in Romans 14 Paul deals with the question of whether Christians could eat meat from animals that had been sacrificed to pagan gods — at dinners for

clubs or guilds held in pagan temples. Paul contends that, because idols are nothing, the meat is not polluted; Christians nevertheless should not give undue offense to their "weaker" co-members.

5. Misconduct during the sacred meal (11:17-34). Paul had received a report that the Christians at Corinth were not properly observing the "Lord's Supper," which at that time was part of a common meal. Wealthier members made a display of their food, eating and drinking to excess, while the poorer members were humiliated. Paul angrily responds to this evidence of factionalism, reminding them of Jesus' somber words to his disciples at the Last Supper (this account of Jesus' last meal antedates the written accounts in Matthew, Mark, Luke, and John). Jesus spoke of the bread as his body and the cup as "the new covenant in my blood." The meal is a repetition of the Last Supper and a proclamation of "the Lord's death" (11:26).

6. Spiritual gifts (Greek: *charismata;* chs. 12–14). The Corinthians were not sure what attitude to take toward speaking in tongues *(glossolalia),* a phenomenon widespread among various religions in the time of Paul. Persons who engaged in the practice believed that they were possessed by the Spirit of God, but some others viewed it as offensive. Paul responds with a series of statements: Glossolalia is a gift of the Spirit, but it must be provided with interpretation (14:6, 13) if it is to be useful to the church, and the content of the messages should be tested (12:1-3). Ultimately, however, one spiritual gift is supreme over all others:

> If I speak with the tongues of mortals and of angels, but do not have love, I am a noisy gong or a clanging cymbal. And if I have prophetic powers, and understand all mysteries and all knowledge, and if I have faith, so as to remove mountains, but do not have love, I am nothing. (13:1-2)

7. The resurrection of the dead (ch. 15). Paul had heard that some Corinthians had questions about his preaching about the resurrection of the dead at the last day. What would happen to them if, at the day of resurrection, they would still be alive while the dead are raised to a

glorious new life (15:51, "We will not all die, but we shall all be changed")? More basically, why is a "body" needed for the next life? The matter is of great significance for Paul because his gospel centered on the proclamation of the crucified *and risen* Jesus. He therefore begins chapter 15 with a summary of the evidence for Jesus' resurrection (vv. 3-11) — a significant text in several respects. Those who affirm Jesus' resurrection must affirm also the resurrection of the believers. Believers will be raised to the same condition as was Jesus — a "spiritual body" (vv. 35-49). Those who are still living when this happens will be instantly transformed into the new body, at which point death will have been eternally vanquished (vv. 50-58).

Romans

Paul's letter to the Romans is the lengthiest of his corpus and the only surviving one he wrote to a church he had not yet visited. As a letter of introduction to inform the church in Rome of his plans to visit them and to enlist their support for a further trip to Spain (Rom. 1:10; 15:22-29), it centers on his understanding of the Christian faith rather than on problems in the Roman congregation.

This letter has a fairly clear organization:

1. Introduction (1:1-17). Paul asserts that he was "set apart" for preaching "the gospel of God," which centers on Jesus who, he says, was "declared to be Son of God with power . . . by resurrection from the dead" (1:4) — dating the manifestation of Jesus' glory later than do the Gospel writers. Typical of the friendly letters of antiquity — and even today — Paul commends his readers and then tactfully informs them of his plans to visit Rome (1:11-15), although he delays telling them of his plans to proceed from Rome to Spain until the end of the letter (15:23-24). Then, in 1:16-17 he turns to the main theme he will develop in the letter, the "righteousness of God" that is "revealed" in the gospel he preaches, and the way a human being can participate in this righteousness. (He expounds his understanding of this concept especially in 3:21–4:25).

2. Human unrighteousness and God's wrath (1:18–3:20). Paul's own personal turn toward the gospel of the crucified and risen Jesus was apparently a bolt from the blue. Insisting that faith in this Jesus was necessary to participate in God's righteousness, he attempts in this section to show that all humans, whether Gentile (1:18-32; 2:12-16) or Jew (2:1-11; 2:17–3:20), fail to attain such status. Polytheism, which led to moral degeneration, and instinctive awareness of what the Law demands reveal the culpability of the Gentiles. The Jews, who have the Law and many other privileges (see also 9:4-5), have condemned Gentile immorality (2:1-11), while their own Scripture, the Old Testament, reveals that no one has been able to match God's righteousness even with knowledge of the Law (3:1-20).

3. The revelation and bestowal of God's righteousness (3:21–4:25). Undoubtedly because of the radical change in his life that stemmed from his vision of the risen Jesus (referred to in Gal. 1:15-16; 1 Cor. 9:1), Paul proclaims that God's righteousness now is bestowed on humans who respond in faith to his message of the risen Christ. He asserts, moreover, that this is "attested by the law and the prophets," that is, the Old Testament. Paul refers especially to Abraham, who is declared in Genesis to have been "reckoned" by God as righteous by virtue of his faith (Rom. 4). It is abundantly clear that Paul saw in the death and resurrection of Jesus a turning point in human history.

4. The results of the bestowal of righteousness (5:1–8:39). If righteousness is bestowed, several questions arise: (a) Are believers free from sin (ch. 6)? Paul's answer is ambiguous: All humans had been slaves of sin, but believers are now "enslaved to God" (6:22). (b) Why did God reveal the Law to the Israelites? Paul's answer to this question is even more ambiguous than that to the former question, and a large number of books have tried to make sense of it. (c) What does it mean, then, to live with the bestowal of righteousness? Paul: Believers live "according to the Spirit" or "in the Spirit," a life that is contrasted with life "according to the flesh." The section ends with a majestic statement of confidence in God (8:31-39).

5. Israel and salvation (9:1–11:36). If God instituted a new plan for humanity in the death and resurrection of Jesus, how can we understand the Old Testament assertions of the prerogatives of Israel, whom God chose as a special people, entered into covenant with, and to whom God gave the Law? Paul tries to show that from the time of Abraham there had always been a predetermined sifting between faithful and unfaithful descendants (9:6-29). This demarcation was confirmed by the concerned persons' responses (10:1-21). Israel as such, however, is not rejected by God. Instead, by some mysterious action or decision of God, "all Israel will be saved" in the end (11:26), so that God's ultimate purpose for the cosmos can be accomplished (11:36).

6. Moral virtues and the good life (12:1–15:13). Although, according to Paul, righteousness is bestowed by God as a gift, believers are to cultivate moral virtues and to be "transformed by the renewing of [their] minds" (12:2). They are to aim for harmony with fellow believers (12:3-8) and (here Paul cites phrases that are reminiscent of Jesus' teaching) cultivate love, hope, and the blessing of their persecutors (12:14-21), including the "authorities" in Rome (13:1-7). Paul ends the body of the book with a carefully worded explanation of his current situation and his firm plans to visit Rome and then Spain (15:22-32).

Romans 16 is largely a list of greetings to persons known to Paul — a mine of information about his contacts and networking skills, the details of which are in many cases obscure.

The Other Letters of the Pauline Corpus

The other letters of the Pauline corpus fall into several categories: (1) The earliest Christian documents that have survived are 1-2 Thessalonians, written as early as 50 C.E. They deal with the hostility the new converts in Thessalonica were experiencing as well as what Paul considered their overreaction to his message of the nearness of the end. (2) Galatians and 2 Corinthians represent Paul at his most passionate, countering attacks on his credentials and his message from opponents, who in Galatians represented a more conservative line of thought with respect to Judaism, and some of whom in Corinth questioned his motives in arranging for a collection of money from them for the poor in Jerusalem. (3) The "prison letters" — Ephesians, Philippians, Colossians, and Philemon — are so called because the author, stated in the letters to have been Paul, claims to be writing while imprisoned for the faith. Paul's short note to Philemon is a prime example of the friendly letter of antiquity, in which Paul pleads for Philemon to exercise compassion and consideration toward his runaway Christian slave, Onesimus. (4) The "pastoral letters" — 1-2 Timothy and Titus — although claiming to have been written by Paul, reflect issues and developments from a later stage in the early church than the life of Paul; they may be dated to the turn of the 1st century or even later.

THE GENERAL LETTERS

Among the so-called general letters of the New Testament — Hebrews, James, 1-2 Peter, 1, 2, and 3 John, and Jude — are common themes of persecution from pagan neighbors and the state (Hebrews, James, 1-2 Peter) and the threat of laxity and dissension within the Christian communities (Hebrews, James, 1-3 John, Jude). The literary style ranges from the most classical of New Testament writings (Hebrews) to folk wisdom (James) and simple Greek (1-3 John). On James, see Chapter 2, above.

Reading Ancient Letters

Crucial to understanding a letter is to know who wrote it, when, to whom, and for what reason. When the occasion for a letter is not fully stated in it — as when Paul in Galatians responds to his opponents or in 1 Corinthians to his rivals — it is necessary to reconstruct the situation on the basis of the arguments presented, like moving from the answer back to the question. This process, however, can result in divergent understandings of the text.

Modern readers can gain a sense of the variety of biblical letters by beginning with one that deals with specific problems, like Jer. 29:4-23 or 1 Corinthians, and then moving to the more formal and abstract letter to the Romans.

As occasional pieces, personal letters might not convey what the author holds to be most important on a given topic but instead respond to specific queries from the addressees. If they are genuine letters, however, they usually convey — even across the centuries — some of the passion and basic convictions of the writer.

9

Redemptive Persuasion: The Gospels

Of all the literary forms in the Bible, the one that has the strongest claim to uniqueness is the Gospel. Numerous attempts have been made during the past two centuries to assess the relationship of the Gospel as literary form with forms known from the Old Testament and from the Hellenistic world. Are the Gospels akin to narrative writings of the Old Testament or to biographical writing of antiquity, such as the lives of Homer and Aesop, those by Plutarch, Greek myths of heroes, and — especially — Philostratus's *Life of Apollonius* (written shortly after 200 C.E.; Apollonius was a 1st-century Greek miracle worker)? Or should we think of memoirs, like Xenophon's of Socrates, or perhaps folk literature without further definition?

All such proposals have ultimately failed to gain a scholarly consensus. The Gospels are unique with respect to the origin of the material and, above all, in their stated attempt to convince readers of the truth of Christian interpretation of the significance of Jesus of Nazareth. Jesus contradicted the Greco-Roman criteria for heroic biography. He was not the ideal philosopher, as portrayed by Plutarch, nor a model political or military leader. Closer analogies can perhaps be found in the development in Judaism of the figure of the "founder," as in the treatment of Moses by the 1st-century Jewish philosopher Philo and the Jewish historian Josephus. The Gospels, however, display the unique purpose of creating faith and trust in the figure of Jesus and therefore must provide their own clues regarding their literary form.

The Origin of the Gospels

The earliest Gospel tradition was oral in form and most probably in the Aramaic language. After his death, followers of Jesus in Jerusalem and in Galilee began to organize their own groups and engage in missionary activity among their neighbors. For such occasions, remembered words of Jesus and reports of his activities were found useful. An additional impetus to preserve the words and deeds of Jesus was the desire to venerate Jesus, narrate the actions that led to his death, demonstrate his unique relationship to God, and bear witness to his resurrection from the dead.

As the group of Jesus' followers spread, the movement early on crossed over to Jews whose native tongue was Greek and then to Greek-speaking non-Jews. At each stage of such transmission, the Gospel tradition evolved and took on more clearly defined subgenres.

Of the several Christian Gospels written during the first two centuries c.e., four are included in the New Testament. All four are anonymous (the names of the authors are not given in their contents but only in the titles, which apparently were appended later). Subsequent early Christian writers, however, made assertions on this matter. I will use the traditional titles as a convenience, without respect to specific views on authorship.

Matthew, Mark, and Luke have a significant amount of common material and share the same basic outline of Jesus' activity. They are therefore known as the "Synoptic" Gospels, which means that they share a "common perspective," different from the Gospel of John, whose outline and contents are highly distinctive, even though subtle reminiscences of the other Gospels can be found in it.

THE SYNOPTIC PROBLEM

The Synoptic problem is that of explaining the similarities and the dissimilarities of content in Matthew, Mark, and Luke. The common material sometimes exhibits verbal identity in the original Greek to the degree that most scholars think that there must have been a literary relationship among them. Did one or two of the Synoptic authors have the text of the one or two others as he or she wrote? If so, which was used by the others? Or did all three Synoptic writers use some of the same sources? During the past two centuries a general consensus on these questions has emerged, along the following lines:

1. The Priority of Mark

Markan priority means that Mark was written prior to and was used as a major source by both Matthew and Luke. Ninety percent of Mark's material recurs in Matthew (a good half of Matthew's content), and 53 percent of Mark recurs in Luke. More significantly, although the sequence of material in Matthew and Luke is not identical, both appear to be following the order of the Markan material. Stylists and exegetes identify numerous common passages in which either Matthew or Luke (or both) appears to make "improvements" of various kinds in his Markan source. (A book of "Gospel Parallels" reveals this at a glance.) For a simple example, compare the wording of the question about fasting:

Matt. 9:14-15	Mark 2:18-20	Luke 5:33-35
Then the disciples of John came to him, saying, "Why do we and the Pharisees fast often, but your disciples do not fast?"	Now John's disciples and the Pharisees were fasting; and people came and said to him, "Why do John's disciples and the disciples of the Pharisees fast, but your disciples do not fast?" Jesus said to them, "The wedding guests cannot fast while the bridegroom is with them, can they? As long as they have the bridegroom with them, they cannot fast. The days will come when the bridegroom is taken away from them, and then they will fast on that day."	Then they said to him, "John's disciples, like the disciples of the Pharisees, frequently fast and pray, but your disciples eat and drink."
And Jesus said to them, "The wedding guests cannot mourn as long as the bridegroom is with them, can they? The days will come when the bridegroom is taken away from them, and then they will fast.		Jesus said to them, "You cannot make wedding guests fast while the bridegroom is with them, can you? The days will come when the bridegroom will be taken away from them, and then they will fast in those days."

2. Non-Markan Material Common to Matthew and Luke

Matthew and Luke have in common approximately 275 verses that are not found in Mark. How can this be explained? It cannot be that either Matthew or Luke knew the work of the other in the form that we have it. The close similarity of much of this material also rules out identical oral traditions transmitted separately. We are left with one hypothesis, which is presupposed by the plurality of scholars today, namely, that Matthew and Luke used a common document in addition to Mark. This document is known as "Q," from the German word *Quelle,* "source." Almost all Q material consists of sayings of Jesus (parables, aphorisms, and the "Lord's Prayer"), with some sayings of John the Baptist. This lack of narrative means also that in Q there is no account of Jesus' death or resurrection. For examples of Q material, compare the account of Jesus' temptation by Satan in Matt. 4:1-11 with Luke 4:1-13 or the two forms of the "Lord's Prayer":

Matt. 6:9-13	Luke 11:2-4
"Pray then in this way:	He said to them, "When you pray, say:
Our Father in heaven, hallowed be your name.	Father, hallowed be your name.
Your kingdom come.	Your kingdom come.
Your will be done, on earth as it is in heaven.	
Give us this day our daily bread.	Give us each day our daily bread.
And forgive us our debts, as we also have forgiven our debtors.	And forgive us our sins, for we ourselves forgive everyone indebted to us.
And do not bring us to the time of trial, but rescue us from the evil one."	And do not bring us to the time of trial."

3. Material Unique to Matthew

Matthew has approximately 230 verses that occur neither in Mark nor in Luke. This includes many parables attributed to Jesus and several narratives with an abundance of quotations or allusions from the Old Testament. This "M" material gives the Gospel of Matthew a strongly Jewish flavor. Did the author have access to written sources besides

Mark and Q? Or does this material come from various oral traditions, including those of the earliest Jerusalem church? An example of M:

> Do not think that I have come to abolish the law and the prophets; I have come not to abolish but to fulfill. For truly I tell you, until heaven and earth pass away, not one letter, not one stroke of a letter, will pass from the law until all is accomplished. Therefore, whoever breaks one of the least of these commandments, and teaches others to do the same, will be called least in the kingdom of heaven; but whoever does them and teaches them will be called great in the kingdom of heaven. For I tell you, unless your righteousness exceeds that of the scribes and Pharisees, you will never enter the kingdom of heaven. (Matt. 5:17-20)

4. Material Unique to Luke

The "L" material amounts to more than 400 verses and includes 14 parables (including the parable of the Prodigal Son) and some 30 narratives. Much of this material is located in the stories of the births of John and Jesus (chs. 1–2) and in a "special section" that Luke inserts into the Markan outline at Luke 9:51–18:14. In this material, Jesus emerges as a prophet who speaks on behalf of the dispossessed and oppressed, undisturbed by apocalyptic fervor. An example of L:

> Now as they went on their way, he entered a certain village, where a woman named Martha welcomed him into her home. She had a sister named Mary, who sat at the Lord's feet and listened to what he was saying. But Martha was distracted by her many tasks; so she came to him and asked, "Lord, do you not care that my sister has left me to do all the work by myself? Tell her then to help me." But the Lord answered her, "Martha, Martha, you are worried and distracted by many things; there is need of only one thing. Mary has chosen the better part, which will not be taken away from her." (Luke 10:38-42)

This solution of the Synoptic problem is often referred to as the "four-source theory" (Mark, Q, M, and L) or the "two-document theory" (Mark and Q). Those who hold to the theory would date Mark about 65-75 c.e. and Q, in written form, somewhat earlier, perhaps 50-60 c.e. One implication of this theory is that none of the Synoptics was written by an original follower of the historical Jesus. It is extremely unlikely that an original follower of Jesus would have used the outline and much of the content of a Gospel from Mark, who was not one of Jesus' first disciples.

BEFORE THE GOSPELS

The four-source theory does not itself explain the origin of the material in Mark, Q, M, or L. The study of the transmission of Gospel materials from the time of the speaking of the sayings and the occurrence of the events described until their being written is known as "form criticism." Form critics study the ways oral tradition is shaped, preserved, and transmitted. With regard to the Synoptic material, form critics assume that

- The material was originally transmitted as independent units, without an overarching framework.
- Individual units were preserved if they served the needs of the emerging church in evangelism, worship, internal discipline, external controversy, and others.
- Collections of words and deeds of Jesus were first made by the earliest Aramaic-speaking Christians in Palestine. They then came to be translated into Greek by early Greek-speaking Jewish Christians and subsequently were further shaped by Gentile Christians.

The Gospels, therefore, are complex documents whose basic purpose is to encourage Christian faith and values. The attempt to determine the actual words and deeds of Jesus from the Gospel materials has become a highly technical and disputed scholarly discipline.

The Gospel of Mark

As the earliest written account of Jesus' activity and a presumed major source of Matthew and Luke, the Gospel of Mark is a historical document of great importance and will be given priority treatment in this chapter. Its contents and themes, moreover, raise basic issues in the quest of the historical Jesus.

The origins of Mark remain a mystery. Early Christian tradition is unanimous that this Gospel was written by John Mark, a follower of Peter (Peter is prominent in Mark's story). Mark is mentioned several times in other books of the New Testament (Acts 12:12, 25; 13:5, 13; 15:37, 39; Col. 4:10-12; 2 Tim. 4:11; Phlm. 24; and 1 Pet. 5:13). This Mark was also a companion of Paul. Later Christian tradition asserts that he was the first bishop of Alexandria in Egypt.

As literature, the Gospel of Mark, both in the original Greek and in translation, is episodic, abrupt in transitions, but gripping and dramatic. The historical present tense recurs, and a sequential flow of individual episodes does not really appear until the account of Jesus' death in Jerusalem (Mark 14–15). The book as a whole, however, exhibits structural organization in two respects.

Mark can be viewed *thematically* as composed of two main sections, with the break between them coming at 8:27. The first half describes Jesus' proclamation of the kingdom of God and some acts of healing in Galilee. Beginning in 8:27, the question of his identity begins to be raised (is he the Messiah? the Son of God in a special sense? or something else?), and his martyrdom in Jerusalem begins to occupy his own sayings and intentions. Three times (8:31; 9:31; 10:33), each time more explicitly, Jesus tells his closest followers that he will soon undergo a violent death.

Mark can also be read in terms of its *geographical progression* from Galilee to Jerusalem, an outline that differs considerably from that of the Gospel of John but which was adopted, with variations, by both Matthew and Luke. According to Mark, Jesus entered Jerusalem only once during his ministry (on the Sunday before his crucifixion), whereas the Gospel of John narrates several trips of Jesus between Galilee and Jerusalem during the entire period of his activity. The sweep of the narrative can be followed in annotated outline form.

INTRODUCTION (MARK 1:1-15)

The opening words of Mark, "The beginning of the good news of Jesus Christ, the Son of God," are probably to be taken in a historical sense. Mark intends to report how Jesus' activity originated historically: the "good news" of Jesus began when Jesus came into contact with John the Baptist.

John the Baptist (Mark 1:4-8; Matt. 3:1-12; Luke 3:2-18)

John appeared in "the wilderness" and baptized people in the Jordan River, apparently not far from Jericho. He wore crude attire and ate available desert food that was considered ritually clean. He urged the crowds to repent of their sins, and he baptized those who did so. The motivation for John's preaching of repentance was his conviction that the eschatological wrath of God would soon be manifest in a judgment like the burning of fruitless trees or the burning of chaff at harvest. John's baptism, therefore, was a public indication that the baptized person was prepared for God's judgment.

Mark (as Matthew and Luke) reports one other aspect of John's message: his reference to a "more powerful" figure to come after him and that he was "not worthy to stoop down and untie the thong of his sandals. I have baptized you with water; but he will baptize you with the Holy Spirit" (Mark 1:7-8). Although in Mark, John does not further identify this figure (leaving the possibility that John might have thought of an unspecified agent of God's judgment), it is clear that the early Christians believed that "the coming one" was Jesus (see John 1:25-27).

Jesus' Baptism

Jesus was baptized by John. This fact was an apparent embarrassment for some early Christians, because John baptized only those who had repented. Matthew inserts into the story of Jesus' baptism a dialogue in which John hesitates to baptize Jesus (Matt. 3:14-15). Jesus' baptism nonetheless shows that he believed John's message and viewed John's activity as God-inspired.

Mark reports that, at his baptism, Jesus "saw the heavens torn apart and the Spirit descending like a dove on him" and that he heard a voice from heaven, "You [second person singular] are my Son, the Beloved; with you I am well pleased!" (Mark 1:10-11; Mark's subjective interpretation of the vision and the voice are altered by Matthew and Luke). Mark appears to understand Jesus' baptism as a radically new stage in his self-awareness. Jesus came to view himself as God's beloved Son and to view his actions henceforth as directed by God's Spirit.

"Immediately" following the baptism, Mark reports, the Spirit drove Jesus into the wilderness, where he was "tempted by Satan" for 40 days, accompanied by wild beasts and ministering angels. The new awareness Jesus gained at his baptism was being put to the test. The air of authority in Jesus' words and deeds, according to Mark, came from the Spirit of God.

Jesus' Proclamation of the Kingdom of God

Mark 1:14-15 functions as a summary of Jesus' message:

> Now after John was arrested, Jesus came to Galilee, proclaiming the good news of God, and saying, "The time is fulfilled, and the kingdom of God has come near; repent, and believe in the good news."

Mark's assertion that Jesus waited to begin his ministry until John's had come to an end suggests that Jesus viewed his own work as a continuation of John's, at least in some respects. Later in Mark, some persons wondered whether Jesus was "John the baptizer . . . raised from the dead" (Mark 6:14).

According to Mark, Jesus' preaching centered on the theme, "the time is fulfilled, and the kingdom of God has come near." In Mark 4:26, 30, and especially 4:11, Jesus introduces his parables with the expression, "The kingdom of God is like. . . ." And, at his last meal with his disciples, he avers that he would "never again drink of the fruit of the vine until that day when I drink it new in the kingdom of God" (Mark 14:25; see also the Q text Matt. 8:11//Luke 13:29). Moreover, at an unspecified point in his activity, Jesus said, "Truly I tell you, there are some standing here who will not taste death until they see that the kingdom of God has come with power" (Mark 9:1). Mark clearly emphasizes a transcendent, supernatural, and eschatological aspect to Jesus' proclamation of the kingdom of God.

The expression "kingdom of God" does have eschatological — if not apocalyptic — overtones in both Jewish and Christian tradition. In essence, it refers to the effectiveness of God's will in creation, including human life. For Jesus, to proclaim the nearness of God's kingdom is essentially no different from praying, "Your will be done, on earth as it is in heaven" (Matt. 6:10). God's kingdom (= God's will) is already perfectly done in heaven but only partially on earth. When evil (whether demons, natural catastrophes, personal transgressions, societal discrimination, human pride, or a host of other examples) is opposed and healing begun, the effective rule or kingdom of God is being extended. Jesus viewed his own activity, both healing and teaching, as an anticipation of the universalizing of God's will. The only question that remains is whether he believed that its total implementation would occur within a very short period of time — before the passing of his generation (see Mark 9:1).

JESUS' ACTIVITY IN AND AROUND GALILEE (MARK 1:16–9:50)

Mark reports that Jesus' activity up to 7:24 centered on a small area around the north shore of the Sea of Galilee, and that Jesus then ventured outside Galilee to the northwest and north. In 7:24, with no explanation for the change, Mark reports that Jesus "set out and went away to the region of Tyre and Sidon," and from there went to "the region of the Decapolis" (7:31), the district of Dalmanutha (8:10), Bethsaida (8:22), then "to the villages of Caesarea Philippi" (8:27), a "high mountain" (9:2), "through Galilee" (9:30), and finally back to Capernaum (9:33). After chapter 9, Jesus did not return to Galilee (but see 16:7). No activity is reported in Judea or in Samaria.

With regard to the activity of Jesus within a few miles of his home in Capernaum (Mark 1:16–8:26), Mark has startling things to say about Jesus' actions and words.

Jesus' Actions

Seventeen narratives in Mark (27 or so in the Synoptic Gospels, not counting parallels separately) can be considered "miracle stories," designated in the text by such terms as "powers," "wonders," "mighty works," and "signs." These can be classified as healings (H), exorcisms (E), nature miracles (N), or resuscitations (R). Here is one way of listing the parallels and of classifying the types.

H	1. Peter's mother-in-law	Mark 1:30-31//Matt. 8:14-15; Luke 4:38-39
E	2. Man with unclean spirit	Mark 1:23-26//Luke 4:33-37
H	3. Cleansing of a leper	Mark 1:40-42//Matt. 8:2-4//Luke 5:12-16
H	4. Healing of a paralyzed man	Mark 2:3-12//Matt. 9:2-8//Luke 5:18-26
H	5. Man with withered hand	Mark 3:1-5//Matt. 12:9-14//Luke 6:6-11
N	6. Stilling of storm	Mark 4:37-39//Matt. 8:23-27// Luke 8:22-25
E	7. Gerasene demoniac	Mark 5:1-13//Matt. 8:28-34//Luke 8:26-39
H/R	8. Jairus's daughter	Mark 5:22-24, 35-42//Matt. 9:18-19, 23-26//Luke 8:40-42, 49-56
H	9. Woman with hemorrhage	Mark 5:25-34//Matt. 9:20-22// Luke 8:43-48
N	10. Feeding of the 5000	Mark 6:35-44//Matt. 14:15-21// Luke 9:12-17

N	11. Walking on the water	Mark 6:45-51//Matt. 14:22-33
H	12. Syrophoenician daughter	Mark 7:25-30//Matt. 15:22-28
H	13. Deaf man healed	Mark 7:32-35
N	14. Feeding of the 4000	Mark 8:1-9//Matt. 15:32-39
H	15. Blind man at Bethsaida	Mark 8:22-26//Matt. 9:27-31// Luke 18:35-43
E	16. Son with speech impediment	Mark 9:17-27//Matt. 17:14-21// Luke 9:38-43
H	17. Blind Bartimaeus	Mark 10:46-52//Matt. 20:30-34// Luke 18:35-43

Religious healing is documented in the Old Testament, in later Jewish documents, and in the Greek world. The first action Mark reports is an exorcism in the synagogue at Capernaum (1:21-28). The demons who possessed the man call Jesus by name and refer to his special status:

> "What have you to do with us, Jesus of Nazareth? Have you come to destroy us? I know who you are, the Holy One of God." (Mark 1:24)

Mark refers to many other healings on that day and adds that "he would not permit the demons to speak, because they knew him" (1:34). Mark contrasts the unknowingness of the disciples with the demons' supernatural knowledge, who make a "Christian" confession before any disciple does (see Mark 5:7). In Mark, Jesus' true identity is concealed from humans until chapter 8.

For Mark, Jesus' acts of healing are not only connected with the question of his identity. They also account for the rapid growth of his reputation and the onset of serious opposition to his activity, especially on the part of scribes (experts in the Torah, 2:6), Pharisees (2:18), and Herodians (3:6). Mark places the threat on Jesus' life as early as 3:6.

With respect to the interpretation of Jesus' actions, Mark 3:22-30 reports that Jesus' opponents ("the scribes who came down from Jerusalem") did not deny that he performed "signs and wonders" — exorcisms in particular — but that they interpreted such as being done by the power of the devil, Beelzebul, the ruler of the demons. Jesus to them was a sorcerer. Jesus, according to Mark, responded with a *reductio ad absurdum:* the prince of demons would not cast out his own assistants. For Mark such activity was evidence of Jesus' authority as the unique Son of God.

Mark reports that Jesus' actions made him well known throughout Galilee, but that they did not create anything like Christian faith in Jesus on the part of the disciples. That is to say, Mark does not depict the Twelve as applying to Jesus titles like Messiah (at least until ch. 8) or Son of God (the Roman soldier does so in 15:39).

Jesus' Sayings (Teachings)

Generally speaking, three kinds of sayings are attributed to Jesus in Mark and the other Synoptics: pronouncement stories (a saying fitted out with a brief narrative frame, such as the scene of Jesus blessing the children in Mark 10:13-16), independent sayings (aphorisms, prophetic sayings, conflict sayings), and parables. There are 60 different parables (some of which are found in more than one Gospel) in the Synoptics, and these amount to approximately one-half of the bulk of the sayings attributed to Jesus in Matthew, Mark, and Luke.

Mark 4 is a brief collection of parables: The Sower (vv. 3-8), The Seed Growing Secretly (vv. 26-29), and The Mustard Seed (vv. 30-32). All of them are stated to be parables of the kingdom of God (vv. 11, 26, 30), but it is almost impossible for modern readers to discern precisely what Jesus intended them to say about this theme. The kingdom will surely come, in spite of obstacles — just as a harvest comes in spite of bad soil, weeds, and pests (The Sower). The "harvest" of the kingdom will appear without it being forced by humans (The Seed Growing Secretly). And Jesus' proclamation of the kingdom, considered by his opponents of little account, will be vindicated by its future fulfillment (The Mustard Seed).

Mark asserts that when Jesus spoke in public of the kingdom of God he used parables, but that he spoke in unambiguous language privately to his own disciples (4:34). (That Jesus distinguished his private instruction from his public speaking is even more clearly emphasized in the Gospel of John.) For Mark, there is a "secret" or "mystery" about the kingdom, and this mystery was to be kept from "those outside":

> When he was alone, those who were around him along with the twelve asked him about the parables. And he said to them, "To you has been given the secret of the kingdom of God, but for those outside, everything comes in parables; in order that
>
>> 'they may indeed look, but not perceive,
>>   and may indeed listen, but not understand;
>> so that they may not turn again and be forgiven.'"
>
> (Mark 4:10-12)

Mark, quoting Isa. 6:9-10, makes the astounding assertion that Jesus spoke in parables to the public for the purpose of *concealing* the mystery of the kingdom of God. Although some have sought to find a place for this in the actual mission of Jesus, Mark was probably thinking retrospectively. Just as the account of Isaiah's call included the "prediction" that his word would not be believed, so Jesus' message was not accepted by the majority of his own people. It is possible, moreover, that Mark was, in part, expressing his own frustration in understanding the point of the parables by asserting that they were intended to conceal rather than communicate.

Mark is primarily a book of action and narrative rather than discourse. Mark nonetheless includes a number of aphorisms of various kinds, as, for example, the sayings in 4:21-25.

Noteworthy in this Galilean section of Mark are sayings attributed to Jesus about the Law of Moses in chapter 7. Jesus' critics here are identified as Pharisees, the most widely distributed Jewish sect in Palestine at that time. Some Pharisees "and some of the scribes who had come from Jerusalem" asked why Jesus' disciples ate without the ceremonial washing of hands. Mark explains that the Pharisees observe "the tradition of the elders," a reference to traditional oral laws that came to be considered as originating with Moses (this "oral Torah" was put into writing around 200 C.E. and called the Mishnah). According to Mark, Jesus declared in this context that "there is nothing outside a person that by going in can defile, but the things that come out are what defile" (Mark 7:15). Perplexed by this statement, which seemed at odds with the distinction in the Pentateuch between "clean" and "unclean" foods, the disciples asked him what he had meant. Jesus, according to Mark, further declared that food cannot defile, but what comes out of the heart — "evil intentions . . . fornication, theft, murder, adultery, avarice, wickedness, deceit, licentiousness, envy, slander, pride, folly. . . defiles a person" (7:21-22). Mark adds an astounding interpretive comment: "Thus he declared all foods clean" (7:19; these words are deleted in the parallel in Matt. 15:1-20). Mark's assertion, perhaps in line with developments in the churches in the second half of the 1st century, interprets Jesus' statements as a contradiction of the written Torah, in which clear distinctions between permissible and forbidden foods are made. (Matthew's more Torah-observant picture of Jesus is quite different.)

Jesus' Identity

In the first eight chapters of Mark, the question of Jesus' identity emerges among the public. Mark offers an overview of reactions (especially to Jesus' healing activity) in 6:14-16:

> King Herod [Antipas, son of Herod the Great] heard of [Jesus], for Jesus' name had become known. Some were saying, "John the baptizer has been raised from the dead; and for this reason these powers are at work in him." But others said, "It is Elijah." And others said, "It is a prophet, like one of the prophets of old." But when Herod heard of it, he said, "John, whom I beheaded, has been raised."

According to Mark, the public impression of Jesus toward the end of his activity in Galilee was that of a significant figure — Jesus might be a prophet like those of ancient times; he might be Elijah, the forerunner of the coming of judgment or of the Messiah (see Mal. 4:5); or he might be John the Baptist *redivivus* (Herod Antipas had recently put John to death). But, presumably, no one — with the important exception of demons, who could refer to Jesus as "Son of the Most High God" (Mark

1:24; see 1:34; 3:11) — had suggested that Jesus might be a messianic figure or uniquely the Son of God. Mark does not clearly indicate what Jesus' disciples thought of him up to this point, except to emphasize their obtuseness.

A turning point regarding the disciples' understanding comes in Mark 8:27-38, the narrative known as "Peter's Confession." On the way to Caesarea Philippi, on the foot of Mount Hermon at the extreme northeast corner of Jewish settlement in Palestine, where there was a shrine to the Greek god Pan, Mark reports that Jesus asked his disciples two questions. To the first, "Who do people say that I am?" the disciples respond with the same list that Mark had given in 6:14-16 (John the Baptist, Elijah, one of the prophets). How to understand the responses to the second question, "But who do you say that I am?" is more difficult.

In Mark, Peter responds, presumably on behalf of the Twelve, "You are the Messiah" (the original Greek of Mark has *christos*, "Christ," which came to be the traditional translation of the Hebrew *mashiach*, "Messiah"). Up to this point in Mark, no one — demons or humans — had expressed such a thought. Nor did there appear to be a reason to think that Jesus of Nazareth was the Messiah or a messianic figure, who was expected to revive the Davidic kingdom in a superlative way, one that involved military campaigns against the enemies of the Jews.

Mark's report of the response to Peter's confession is equally startling. First, Jesus "sternly ordered them not to tell anyone about him" (8:30). The theme of secrecy — about the kingdom of God and about Jesus' identity — is a strong and perplexing Markan emphasis.

Mark reports that Jesus then made an astounding announcement to his disciples. He gave his first "passion prediction," telling them that he (the "Son of Man") "must undergo great suffering, and be rejected by the elders, the chief priests, and the scribes, and be killed, and after three days rise again. He said this all quite openly" (8:31-32). Peter privately rebuked Jesus for these thoughts, but Jesus turned to the other disciples and rebuked Peter in the harshest possible language: "Get behind me, Satan! For you are setting your mind not on divine things but on human things" (8:33). Jesus then told his disciples that his followers must be prepared to face the same fate as awaited him in Jerusalem: "If any want to become my followers, let them deny themselves and take up their cross and follow me" (8:34).

Whatever Mark thought that Peter had in mind when he confessed Jesus to be the Messiah, it did not involve the idea of Jesus' imminent sufferings and death. Did Mark attribute to Peter the traditional concept of messiahship in Jewish sources — a Davidic warrior who establishes a universal kingdom of peace and justice headquartered in Jerusalem — which Jesus rejected for himself? Did Jesus repudiate Peter's understanding of Jesus? Whatever the case, Mark's story of Jesus has now taken a decisive turn — from Galilee to Jerusalem, from proclamation of the kingdom of God to a martyr's death, from prophetic teaching of God's will to eschatology.

Among the titles used of Jesus in Mark by various individuals or groups, both friendly and hostile, are: Christ (Messiah), Son of God, "my Son, the Beloved," the Holy One of God, Son of Man, Teacher, Son of the Most High God, prophet, Son of David, Rabbi, Son of the Blessed One, the man from Nazareth, a Galilean, King of the Jews, and King of Israel. The nuances of meaning attached to these terms have filled the pages of numerous scholarly tomes. Of these, three are perhaps most significant for our understanding of the Synoptic Gospels:

- *Messiah:* Why and how the earliest Christians could apply to Jesus a title that seemed to fit his activity so little and yet that became Jesus' functional surname (Christ) is a difficult question. It was claimed (by Matthew, Luke, and possibly, in 10:47, by Mark) that Jesus was descended from David, but he never entertained a military role for himself and appears to have had little interest in politics. Most important, the idea of a suffering Messiah — the essential view of Jesus among many early Christians — appears to have been unknown to any group in Judaism at the time of the origin of Christianity.
- *Son of God:* In Mark and the other Synoptics, this title is rarely found in sayings of Jesus. The only possibilities in Mark are (1) the parable of the Vineyard (12:1-11//Matt. 21:33-46//Luke 20:9-19), in which the "son" might be intended as an analogy to Jesus, and

(2) the strange saying in Mark 13:32, in which Jesus says about the apocalyptic coming of the Son of Man, "But about that day or hour no one knows, neither the angels in heaven, nor the Son, but only the Father." Some scholars have sought to gain a sense of Jesus' own awareness of sonship with God by examining his address of God as "Father" in his individual prayers. This occurs four times in Mark, eight or nine in Q, 23 times in uniquely Matthean passages, six in L, and 107 times in the Gospel of John. Like all early Christians, Mark depicts Jesus as Son of God.

- *Son of Man:* The question of Jesus' possible use of this term and what he might have had in mind are too complex to describe here. Explanations include the contention that he never used the term as a self-designation, that he spoke of another figure shortly to come as the agent of judgment, or perhaps that he creatively combined the Jewish traditions of Suffering Servant, Messiah, and Son of Man.

The story of Jesus being transfigured on a high mountain in the presence of the inner circle of three disciples, Peter, James, and John (Mark 9:2-8//Matt. 17:1-8//Luke 9:28-36), follows the narrative of Peter's Confession of Jesus as Messiah. Mark treats it as a sequel, reporting that it took place "six days later" (9:2). In what sense is it a sequel? Attention must be given to the appearance of Moses and Elijah and to the voice that, as at Jesus' baptism, comes from heaven.

Mark records that Jesus, on a mountain, a typical place of divine epiphany in the Bible, was "transfigured," and his clothes became glisteningly white. There appeared to him Elijah and Moses, representatives of the first two sections of the Hebrew Bible, the Torah and the Prophets. Moreover, according to Jewish traditions, based on Old Testament statements, neither Moses nor Elijah had died but were taken directly to the presence of God and could thus again appear to humans. Stupefied by Jesus having a conversation with Moses and Elijah as peers and at a loss for words, Peter made a clumsy proposal that three booths be erected as a memorial to this occurrence. The voice from heaven came as a corrective to Peter's response: the divine voice announced to the three disciples (the announcement is in the third person, not the second, as at the baptism), "This is my Son, the Beloved; listen to him!" The disciples were to learn that Jesus is even greater than the two Old Testament heroes; he, more than Moses and Elijah, was to be the basis of their belief.

For Mark the Transfiguration thereby confirms that Jesus is either not the Messiah or more than Messiah. He is God's unique Son and the final source of God's revelation. This finality is further confirmed by Jesus' saying in 9:13 that Elijah, the forerunner, had already come (that is, in the person of John the Baptist). Thus, in Mark 8:27–9:9 there are three questions and answers about Jesus' identity:

- "Who do *people* say that I am?" (8:27). The answer: a prophet, Elijah or John.
- "Who do *you* say that I am?" (8:29). The answer: Messiah.
- Who does *God* say that I am? The answer: God's beloved Son (9:7).

Mark's description of Jesus' Galilean activity comes to an end with the story of the healing of an epileptic boy, the second passion prediction, and various disputes.

JESUS' MOVE FROM GALILEE TO JERUSALEM (MARK 10)

In Mark, Jesus journeys to Jerusalem only once after his mission has begun, and the purpose is to suffer there and be put to death. Jesus leaves Galilee at the beginning of chapter 10 and arrives at Jericho at the end. Chapter 11 opens with the entry of Jesus into Jerusalem riding a colt. (In the Gospel of John, Jesus during his ministry moves back and forth between Jerusalem and Galilee.)

Mark inserts into this trip narrative several significant vignettes. In one of them, regarding divorce, Jesus contrasts the primordial will of God as revealed at creation with the compromising nature of the Law of Moses, adjusted to the realities of actual life in this world (10:2-12). He blesses the children (10:13-16), gives economic advice to a rich young man (10:17-31), gives his third and last passion prediction (10:32-34), comments on a turf battle between James and John (10:35-45), and heals blind Bartimaeus (10:46-52).

JESUS' LAST WEEK, IN JERUSALEM (11:1–15:47)

Chapters 11–13

Mark 11–13, set in and around Jerusalem during the last days before Jesus' crucifixion, is essentially a collection of controversy narratives and dialogues that function to explain the reasons for the hostility against Jesus that led to his death. The conflict centers on the question of Jesus' authority to speak and act, especially his assumed authority to interpret the Torah and his prediction of disaster for the nation and the destruction of the temple.

The section opens with Jesus' "triumphal entry" into Jerusalem on what Christians have come to call Palm Sunday (Mark 11:1-10//Matt. 21:1-11//Luke 19:28-40//John 12:12-19), although only the Gospel of John reports that the branches flung by the people in the vanguard of Jesus' entry were palms. It is not clear how Mark (or Jesus) understood this event. Mark reports that the crowds shouted extravagant praise that included the hope for the restoration of David's kingdom, a messianic idea: "Hosanna! Blessed is the one who comes in the name of the Lord!" (11:9)

The material in Mark 11–13 is set mainly in the area of the temple in Jerusalem (11:11, 15, 27; 12:41; 13:1). Jesus' first public action in Jerusalem was directed against those involved in the sale of sacrificial animals in the temple area (11:15-19). Moreover, Jesus' final instruction of the disciples in the Gospel, the "Little Apocalypse" (Mark 13), takes its point of departure from Jesus' prediction of the destruction of the temple. These texts are notoriously difficult to understand, but Jesus was accused by several witnesses at his hearing before the high priest (Mark 14:57-58) of speaking against the temple.

The controversy stories in this section name as antagonists of Jesus "the chief priests, the scribes, and the elders" (11:27), "some Pharisees and some Herodians" (12:13), and "some Sadducees" (12:18) — representatives of the range of religious authorities in Jerusalem.

Mark 13 is a collection of sayings attributed to Jesus about the fate of the temple and the end-events. It contains many features typical of Jewish apocalypses, including the "desolating sacrilege" (v. 14), the darkening of the sun (v. 24), falling stars, the "birthpangs of the Messiah," and others, although it makes no mention of other typical features, such as the casting down of Satan, the last judgment, and the destruction of evil.

Mark 13 opens with Jesus' categorical prediction of the destruction of the temple:

> As he came out of the temple, one of his disciples said to him, "Look, Teacher, what large stones and what large buildings!" Then Jesus asked him, "Do you see these great buildings? Not one stone will be left here upon another; all will be thrown down." (Mark 13:1-2)

This prediction leads to Jesus' statements about the coming of the end of history as we know it. Did Mark believe that the end would come in connection with the Jewish-Roman War, which led to the destruction of the temple in 70 c.e.? Four disciples ask *when* the temple would be destroyed. Jesus responds by predicting that false religious leaders would rise, along with war, earthquakes, and famines, which would be the "beginning of the birthpangs" (that is, either of the messianic age or of the kingdom of God). Following these things, the disciples are to expect persecution and the evangelization of "all nations" (Gentiles).

Mark 13:14-23 suggests that Mark was aware of the Jewish-Roman War — or at least that it was threatening. He refers in v. 14 to the "desolating sacrilege set up where it ought not to be" (a reference to Dan. 9:27; 11:31; 12:11), which must refer to the profanation of the temple, and warns the disciples to flee to the mountains when they see it. After this sacrilege will come the apocalyptic end, with cosmic signs and the coming of the Son of Man "in clouds and with great power and glory" to "gather his elect from the four winds." A perplexing word is added, "Truly I tell you, this generation will not pass away until all these things have taken place" (v. 30). At face value, this means that the end would occur before Jesus' generation had died out; it is possible, however, that Mark had in mind his own generation. Mark 13:30 presents problems identical to those raised by Mark 9:1 ("Truly, I say to you, there are some standing here who will not taste death before they see the kingdom of God come with power," RSV). In Mark, Jesus himself does not know the precise date of the end, but he gives the prerequisites for the coming of the end and counsels his disciples to watch vigilantly.

The Passion Narrative (Mark 14–15)

Chronology Mark 14:12–15:47 is set on the day of Jesus' crucifixion and the day prior to it, that is, Thursday and Friday. Note the following time references:

- "It was two days before the Passover and the festival of Unleavened Bread" (14:1). Passover is a one-day festival that begins at sundown on the evening of the first full moon after the spring equinox (in the Jewish calendar, this is Nisan 15). Unleavened Bread is a week-long festival, the first day of which coincides with the Day of Passover.
- "On the first day of Unleavened Bread, when the Passover lamb is sacrificed . . ." (14:12). On the evening of this day, the Passover would begin. Mark (followed by Matthew and Luke, but not by John) asserts that Jesus' Last Supper with his disciples was eaten on the evening of that day (14:17).
- "As soon as it was morning," Jesus was handed over to Pilate (15:1).
- Jesus was crucified at 9 A.M. (15:25).
- Jesus died shortly after noon (15:33).
- The evening of the day of Jesus' death was the beginning of the Sabbath (Friday evening up to Saturday evening) (15:42).

Mark thus places all the events narrated in 14:12 through 15:47 (the Last Supper through the burial of Jesus) in the space of time from sundown Thursday to sundown Friday. He asserts, moreover, that this day was Passover. (The Gospel of John insists that the day of Passover that year began immediately after the burial of Jesus, and that Jesus was crucified at the time of the slaying of the Passover lambs; see John 18:28; 19:14, 31.)

The Last Supper   After mentioning Judas's intention to betray Jesus — without informing us of the nature of or motivation for it — Mark describes Jesus' Last Supper with his disciples. He asserts that it was the Passover meal that year (Mark 14:12, 14), implying that all the events from this point to the burial of Jesus (the hearing before the Jewish leaders, the hearing before Pilate, the preparations for the execution, and the crucifixion itself) took place on the day of Passover, when the Sabbath laws were in effect. Moreover, Mark does not mention central aspects of the Passover meal, including the lamb and the bitter herbs.

For Mark and all early Christians, the Last Supper was significant especially as the model for the Christian observance of the "Lord's Supper" or Eucharist. The "words of institution" attributed to Jesus at the Last Supper are recorded by all three Synoptic writers and also by Paul (Mark 14:22-25//Matt. 26:26-29//Luke 22:15-20//1 Cor. 11:23-25).

In Mark, Jesus says of the bread, "Take; this is my body," and of the cup, "This is my blood of the covenant, which is poured out for many." The eschatological saying follows immediately, "Truly I tell you, I will never again drink of the fruit of the vine until that day when I drink it new in the kingdom of God." What is Mark's understanding of the significance of the Last Supper?

- It was a fellowship meal, planned by Jesus as the last he would have in this life with his disciples. "All" are to partake, and the thought of Jesus' imminent martyrdom dominated the conversation.
- The eschatological saying, which has a parallel in 1 Cor 11:26 and closer parallels in Matthew and Luke, suggests that Mark viewed the Last Supper as an anticipation of fellowship in the kingdom of God. Immediately before his death, Jesus promised his disciples that in the next life the fellowship they had on earth would be continued.
- Mark emphasizes also the concept of the covenant: "This is my

blood of the covenant, which is poured out for many," a phrase that has clear echoes of Exodus 24, the account of the sacrifice that ratified the covenant with Moses ("See the blood of the covenant that YHWH has made with you in accordance with all these words," Exod. 24:8). Mark views the death of Jesus as a sacrifice that ratifies a new covenant with God, intended for all people.

The Garden   In the Markan narrative, Jesus and his 11 disciples, after the customary hymn of the Passover meal, went to the Mount of Olives, where he predicted Peter's betrayal and his own posthumous appearance to Peter in Galilee (the latter points ahead to Mark 16:7).

Jesus' arrest is narrated in Mark 14:43-52. It is not certain who gave the command for the arrest. All three Synoptics mention that a "crowd" came from "the chief priests, the scribes, and the elders," groups mentioned in the passion predictions (Mark 14:43). The Gospel of John suggests Roman involvement already at this point: "A detachment of soldiers together with police from the chief priests and the Pharisees" (John 18:3; see also 18:12). All Synoptics agree, however, that the Jewish authorities first took custody of Jesus. The disciples all flee, but Mark adds that an unnamed person drew his sword and cut off the ear of a slave of the high priest (14:47) and that a "young man" who followed, "wearing nothing but a linen cloth," dropped the cloth and fled.

The Hearings   In the account of Jesus before the "whole council" of Jewish leaders (Mark 14:53-72), Mark inserts the narrative of Jesus before Caiaphas into the story of Peter's denial, again highlighting the faithlessness of the prince of the apostles.

Mark mentions two meetings of the Jewish council, one in 14:55-65 and the other in 15:1, the first presumably to hear the evidence, reach a verdict, and decide on the sentence; the second to decide what to do next. Because of the sparseness and difficulty of the sources, we cannot determine whether what Mark describes as happening in the hearing before Caiaphas contradicted the legal conventions of Palestinian Judaism of Jesus' time.

Mark records two specific charges against Jesus at the hearing before

Caiaphas: Jesus' sayings about the temple and blasphemy. Testimony was sought against Jesus by "the chief priests and the whole council," but there were found only "many" who "gave false testimony against him, and their testimony did not agree" (14:55-56). But "some stood up and gave false testimony against him, saying, 'We heard him say, "I will destroy this temple that is made with hands, and in three days I will build another, not made with hands."' But even on this point their testimony did not agree" (14:57-59). According to Mark, Jesus did not respond to this charge. The first problem this passage presents is that in Mark 13:1-2 Jesus did in fact predict the destruction of the temple. In what sense, therefore, was the charge false? If the charge in Mark 14:58 is meant to be derived from the statements in 13:2, that is, as the literal destruction of the building itself, then the charge is false in the sense that Jesus did not say that he himself would destroy the temple. The exact same charge, however, recurs in 15:29. If the saying attributed to Jesus by the witnesses in 14:58 is taken as a reference to the new order over against the old order, then, from a Christian point of view, the charge is true: Jesus would create a new order (a new community) at the resurrection on Easter morning (this seems to be the meaning attached to the saying in John 2:19-22). (The temple charge is almost identical to the charge leveled against Stephen, the first Christian martyr, in Acts 6:11-14.) In sum, there is good reason to believe that the historical Jesus did predict the destruction of the Jerusalem temple; it was destroyed by the Romans in August 70 c.e.

The charge of blasphemy also presents acute difficulties. All three Synoptics report that the high priest, unable to get unanimous testimony, asked Jesus whether he was the Messiah (Christ), the "Son of the Blessed One" (Mark 14:61). What was the response? This is one of the few occurrences of Matthew and Luke agreeing against Mark:

- Mark: "Jesus said, 'I am'" (14:62)
- Matthew: "You have said so" (26:64)
- Luke divides the question in two: "'If you are the Messiah, tell us.' He replied, 'If I tell you, you will not believe'" (22:67); "'Are you, then, the Son of God?' He said to them, 'You say that I am.'" (22:70)

This passage, the only place in the Gospel of Mark where Jesus allows himself to be called Messiah without qualification, seems to function as the revelation of the "messianic secret" in Mark. But why do Matthew and Luke disagree with Mark on the response? We cannot know. All three Synoptics, however, agree that Jesus went on to tell the council that they would see "the Son of Man seated at the right hand of the Power, and coming with the clouds of heaven" (Luke omits the last phrase). Mark continues, "Then the high priest tore his clothes and said, 'Why do we still need witnesses? You have heard his blasphemy! What is your decision?' All of them condemned him as deserving death" (Mark 14:63-64).

Why, according to Mark, did the high priest think that Jesus had committed blasphemy? There is no evidence that a messianic claim in itself would have been considered blasphemous at that time. The accusation could be explained in either of two ways: (1) Jesus asserts that he is the Son of Man of Dan. 7:13 who would appear with the clouds of heaven to judge humankind — a reversal of his position before those who were judging him. (2) Jesus' response, "I am" (Greek: *ego eimi*), might have been understood by Mark as a veiled allusion to the divine name, as these words appear to function in the Greek text of Mark 6:50 and, especially, of John 8:24; 18:5-6.

The only charge against Jesus mentioned in Mark's account of Jesus with Pilate (Mark 15:1-15) is that Jesus claimed to be King of the Jews:

- "Pilate asked him, 'Are you the King of the Jews?'" (15:2).
- Pilate "answered them, 'Do you want me to release for you the King of the Jews?'" (15:9).
- "Pilate spoke to them again, 'Then what do you wish me to do with the man you call the King of the Jews?'" (15:12).
- The soldiers "clothed him in a purple cloak; and after twisting some thorns into a crown, they put it on him. And they began saluting him, 'Hail, King of the Jews!'" (15:17-18).
- "The inscription [on the cross] of the charge against him read, 'The King of the Jews'" (15:26).
- The chief priests and some scribes mocked him, "Let the Messiah, the King of Israel, come down from the cross now" (15:32).

Pilate was a Roman pagan, uninterested in Jewish religious traditions. The charges mentioned at the hearing before the Jewish council are here translated into terms meaningful for Pilate. In other words, Mark presents Jesus as being handed over to the Romans as a potentially dangerous political pretender. This is further confirmed by the Barabbas incident in Mark 15:6-15. Mark asserts that Barabbas was a "rebel" in prison and had "committed murder during the insurrection" (the definite article shows that Mark was referring to a specific incident that, unfortunately, is unknown to us). Barabbas was imprisoned for political insurrection, similar to the charge made against Jesus.

The Crucifixion and Death of Jesus   Jesus was mocked as King of the Jews by the soldiers in "the courtyard of the palace (that is, the governor's headquarters)," the Antonia fortress. It was common for Romans to scourge condemned criminals before they were crucified. All three Synoptics mention Simon of Cyrene as the one who carried the cross, but only Mark mentions the names of his sons, Alexander and Rufus, persons undoubtedly known to the first readers of Mark. Mark and Luke add that Simon was "coming in from the country," a detail difficult to explain if this was the day of Passover.

The place: *Golgotha* in Aramaic means "skull"; the Latin translation is Calvary (Greek: *kranions*). Christian legend already from the time of Origen (about 200 C.E.) held that the site of Jesus' crucifixion was precisely the place where Adam had been buried (earlier Jewish tradition held that God took the dust to create Adam's body from what would become the Temple Mount in Jerusalem), so that the blood of Jesus covered the body of Adam. This site was outside the city walls at that time (Heb. 13:12; John 19:20), and there is good reason to believe that it was at the place where the Church of the Holy Sepulchre now stands. In any case, the Romans executed people in public — and especially at places where people gathered, like a crossroads or a theater.

Mark 15:25 asserts that Jesus was crucified at 9 A.M. (Greek: "the third hour"; John 19:14 reads "about noon": Greek: "the sixth hour"), and that there was darkness over the land from noon to 3 P.M. (Greek: "from the sixth to the ninth hour"), according to which Jesus was on the cross for six hours. Whether this was the day of Passover (so Mark) or the day prior (so John) cannot be ascertained. In spite of numerous attempts, these differences between Mark and John cannot be harmonized.

The actual crucifixion is mentioned so briefly as to be amazing. Mark includes the following details:

- The dividing of Jesus' garments, customary in Roman crucifixions (15:24).
- Two "bandits" crucified with Jesus, both of whom "taunted him" (15:27, 32).
- Two miraculous prodigies, darkness at noon (15:33) and the tearing of the temple curtain (15:38), both of which appear to have symbolic significance. The first might be influenced by Old Testament texts. Cf. Amos 8:9, "On that day, says YHWH God, I will make the sun go down at noon, and darken the earth in broad daylight." Whether Mark thought the temple curtain in question was that which separated the Holy Place from the Holy of Holies is not clear, but the tearing of it is given a symbolic interpretation in Heb. 10:19-20.
- Mark (and Matthew) have only one articulate saying of Jesus from the cross, the "cry of dereliction," "My God, my God, why have you forsaken me?" (Mark 15:34), a quotation of Ps. 22:1.
- At the death of Jesus, a centurion said, "Truly this man was God's Son" (15:39; the Greek, lacking the definite article, could be translated, ". . . a son of God"). A Gentile makes a "Christian" confession that stands in sharp contrast to the reviling of Jesus (15:29, 31). Earlier in Mark, Jesus is referred to as Son of God by demons and by the divine voice, but the term is here used for the first time by a human being.
- Mark's Passion Narrative as a whole contains many Old Testament allusions, especially from the Psalms and from Zechariah:

  Mark 14:11, betrayal money: Zech. 11:12
  Mark 14:18, Judas's betrayal: Ps. 41:9

Mark 14:24, blood of the covenant: Exod. 24:8; Zech. 9:11

Mark 14:27, "strike the shepherd": Zech. 13:7

Mark 14:34, Jesus' lament in Gethsemane: Pss. 42:6, 11; 43:5

Mark 15:23, wine mixed with myrrh: Ps. 69:21

Mark 15:24, dividing clothes and casting lots: Ps. 22:18

Mark 15:29, mocking: Pss. 22:7; 109:25

Mark 15:34, cry of dereliction: Ps. 22:1

Mark 15:36, sponge with sour wine: Ps. 69:21

- According to Mark, no male disciples witnessed the crucifixion, but "many" women, some of whom had served Jesus in Galilee, witnessed his death (15:40-41). Three of these women would visit Jesus' tomb on Sunday morning, to anoint his body (16:1).

Jesus' burial, according to Mark, was arranged by "a respected member of the council," Joseph of Arimathea (15:43), immediately prior to the beginning of the Sabbath at sundown that day. Joseph had to visit Pilate, purchase supplies, and perform the burial itself in a short period of time. Pilate, amazed that Jesus had died so quickly (the Jewish historian Josephus, who witnessed mass crucifixions, reports that death from crucifixion sometimes took two or even three days), took steps to confirm the report before granting Joseph permission to bury Jesus (15:44-45). (This was important to the early Christians to counter the rumor that Jesus had not really died.)

THE EMPTY TOMB (MARK 16:1-8)

New Testament reports of the resurrection of Jesus are of two kinds: announcements made at the discovery of Jesus' empty tomb and appearances of the risen Jesus to his followers. On the assumption that the Gospel of Mark originally concluded at 16:8 (see below), it is difficult to explain why only the empty tomb is reported in this Gospel (the young man at the tomb does make a prediction that the risen Jesus would appear to Peter and the other disciples in Galilee [16:7]).

The discovery of the empty tomb is reported in all four Gospels, with curious differences of detail regarding:

- The names and number of women who visited the tomb (Mark mentions three by name — two Marys and Salome; Matthew: the two Marys; Luke: at least five; John: Mary Magdalene only [but she uses the pronoun "we" in 20:2])
- The degree of darkness when the women arrived (Mark: "when the sun had risen"; John: "while it was still dark")
- Why the women went to the tomb (Mark and Luke: to anoint the body; Matthew: to see the tomb; John: unspecified)
- The figure or figures the women saw at the tomb (Mark: "a young man"; Matthew: "an angel of the Lord"; Luke: "two men"; John: "two angels")
- The conversation between the figure(s) and the women
- What the women then did (Mark: "they said nothing to anyone, for they were afraid"; Matthew: "they left the tomb quickly with fear and great joy, and ran to tell his disciples"; Luke: "they told all this to the eleven and to all the rest"; John: "Mary Magdalene went and announced to the disciples, 'I have seen the Lord'")

Various theories have been suggested to account for these differences and for the origin of the empty tomb tradition as a whole. Suggestions that the women visited the wrong tomb ("He is not here") or that Jesus had not really died, awakened, and left or that the disciples invented the story as a fraud are not convincing. Mary Magdalene is the common factor in all versions of the story. Mark's narrative appears to be the basis of the others, and it coheres with the genuine and universal conviction of all of the earliest Christians that God had raised Jesus from the dead and brought him to the presence of God.

The Christian belief in the exaltation of Jesus by God, however, is not identical with belief in the empty tomb, which leads merely to the conviction that the body of Jesus was not there. How the early Christians understood the fate of Jesus is seen most especially in (1) the report of the figure or figures at the tomb and (2) stories of the appearances of the risen Jesus to his followers. The climax of Mark's Gospel is the report of the young man:

> "Do not be alarmed; you are looking for Jesus of Nazareth, who was crucified. He has been raised; he is not here. Look, there is the place they laid him. But go, tell his disciples and Peter that he is going ahead of you to Galilee; there you will see him, just as he told you." (Mark 16:6-7)

Mark's final word, however, has for centuries left readers perplexed:

> So they [the three women] went out and fled from the tomb, for terror and amazement had seized them; and they said nothing to anyone, for they were afraid. (Mark 16:8)

Amazingly, Mark reports that the women were silent, in spite of the young man's command that they "tell his disciples and Peter." The Greek text of Mark 16:8 is even more startling, for it ends with a conjunction. Nowhere else in ancient literature does a book come to an end with a conjunction.

Many early Christians found it intolerable that Mark would end at 16:8. Ancient manuscripts contain a number of alternate endings to the Gospel of Mark. Most late manuscripts include vv. 9-20, the "longer ending," which exhibit a non-Markan style and which mention three appearances of the risen Jesus, a commission reminiscent of the last verses of Matthew, a general report of miracles to be performed by Jesus' followers, and the ascension of Jesus. A major problem is that the longer ending does not supply what 16:7 promises — an appearance of Jesus to the disciples in Galilee. The passage is not found in any of the oldest manuscripts of Mark, and it is cited expressly for the first time by the Christian scholar Irenaeus about 185 C.E. It is clear that if Mark did not originally end at 16:8, the original ending has been lost. The strongest probability remains the theory that Mark intended his Gospel to end with 16:8.

What, then, did the author have in mind in ending the Gospel with the report of the women's silence? We cannot know, but it is consistent with the irony found throughout his work — the obtuseness of the disciples, the anticipation of the culmination of things, the forward momentum, and the "mystery" (4:11) and secrecy that surround Jesus and his message.

The Gospel of Matthew

An old, anonymous jingle conveys some of the distinctive features of the Gospel of Matthew:

> Matthew gives us five discourses;
>> in threes and sevens he likes his sources.
> He writes to show what the Old Testament meant,
>> with an ecclesiastical bent.

1. The most distinctive thing about Matthew's structure is the arrangement of many of Jesus' sayings into five "discourses":

- Chapters 5–7, the Sermon on the Mount
- 9:36–10:42, the mission of the Twelve
- Chapter 13, parables
- 17:22–18:35, church administration
- Chapters 23–25, eschatology (a combination of two discourses)

The narratives that precede each discourse form an outline of five "books," with the birth stories (chs. 1–2) functioning as a preamble or prologue and the Passion Narrative (chs. 26–28) as an epilogue. That this arrangement is intentional is indicated by the fact that the author concludes each of these discourses with a stereotyped formula (7:28; 11:1; 13:53; 19:1; 26:1). The classic explanation of this is that Matthew intended to write a counterpart to the Pentateuch, thereby suggesting that Jesus is a new Moses.

2. A "Jewish Gospel"? Matthew is replete with quotations from the

Old Testament and with reference to Jewish customs and expressions that are mentioned without explanation (hand washing, 15:2; phylacteries and fringes, 23:5; straining gnats, 23:24; whitewashed tombs, 23:27; Hebrew terms are untranslated in 5:22 and 27:6). He recasts phrases in a rabbinic direction ("Is it lawful for a man to divorce his wife *for any cause?*" 19:3; see also 5:32 and 19:9). He emphasizes the unconditional and permanent validity of the Torah (Jewish Law; 5:19; 23:3). He changes Mark's "kingdom of God" to "kingdom of heaven," revealing Jewish sensitivity to the mentioning of God. And he (and no other Gospel writer) asserts that Jesus restricted his mission to Jews (10:5-6, 23; 15:24). The arrangement of smaller units into groups of threes and sevens is also a Jewish tradition.

3. A "Gentile Gospel"? The author emphasizes that Jesus' message is for all peoples: "The field is the world" (13:38); "Make disciples of all nations [Gentiles]" (28:19); "This good news of the kingdom will be proclaimed throughout the world, as a testimony to all the nations [Gentiles]" (24:14); see also 22:9. For Matthew, Jesus' mission to the Jews becomes a universal mission at Jesus' resurrection; in this respect, Matthew appears to share Paul's view that the Christian gospel was first proclaimed exclusively to Jews and then also to the Gentiles (Rom. 1:16).

Some have thought it impossible to imagine anyone of Jewish birth inserting into the Passion Narrative a curse on the Jewish people (Matt. 27:25) or writing in 21:43 that "the kingdom of God will be taken away from you and given to a people that produces the fruits of the kingdom." In addition, many of the "Jewish" aspects of Matthew are not found in editorial material but in the sources used by the author.

4. The Gospel of the church. Matthew is the only Gospel author to use the Greek word *ekklesia,* "church" ("You are Peter, and on this rock I will build my church," 16:18; "If a member refuses to listen . . . tell it to the church," 18:17). Matthew is acutely concerned with church morality (not only in chs. 5–7, the Sermon on the Mount), church structure and discipline (16:17-19; 18:15-20), and church liturgy (the "Lord's Prayer," 6:9-13; a baptismal hymn, 11:25-30; the baptismal formula, 28:16-20).

5. The Gospel of righteousness. Matthew in the Sermon on the Mount (chs. 5–7), especially in the "antitheses" of 5:21-48, offers examples of God's will uncompromised by concessions to the realities of earthly life. This emphasis on higher righteousness (5:20) is found throughout Matthew, although the author is concerned also with practical rules for his community (see, for example, 18:15-18). Matthew's concern with God's will, morality, personal righteousness, good works, and virtue in general is consistent with the description of Jesus as a new Moses who brings a new interpretation of Torah.

6. The apocalyptic Gospel. Matthew was dominated by the thought of judgment, with rewards for the righteous and eternal punishment for evildoers. References to "unquenchable fire" (already in the preaching of John, 3:12; see also 7:19; 13:40, 50; 18:8, 9; 25:41), "gnashing of teeth" (8:12; 13:42, 50; 22:13; 24:51; 25:30), and a universal separation of humanity at the last judgment, related to their works of compassion in earthly life (25:31-46), are based on the familiar Jewish conception of the "two ways," which lead either to eternal punishment or to eternal life (25:46). The last discourse in Matthew (chs. 24–25) surveys the events leading to the end and the final judgment.

These themes can be found already in Matthew's unique stories of Jesus' birth, chapters 1–2. Jesus' genealogy is divided into three groups of fourteen (1:1-17). Gentile Magi visit the infant Jesus in Bethlehem (2:1-12). And five "formula citations" interpret events in the birth story as "fulfillment" of Old Testament passages (1:22-23; 2:5-6; 2:15; 2:17-18; 2:23).

Perhaps the best known of all New Testament texts is the Sermon on the Mount (Matt. 5–7), which includes the "Beatitudes" (5:3-12), the "Antitheses" (examples of Jesus intensifying Old Testament laws, 5:17-48), the "Lord's Prayer" (6:9-13), and miscellaneous commands and virtues to be practiced. These passages, among many others in Matthew, strongly emphasize righteousness, both personal and social.

The universalistic thrust of Matthew is revealed in the final passage (28:16-20), an appearance of the risen Jesus to his disciples in Galilee (unique to Matthew), in which the exalted Jesus, claiming all authority from God, commands his followers to "make disciples of all nations

[= Gentiles]." His promise, "I am with you always, to the end of the age," harks back to 18:20 and also to 1:23, where the baby Jesus is named Emmanuel, "God is with us."

The Gospel of Luke

Almost all scholars today agree that Luke and Acts, the two longest books of the New Testament, were written by the same person. Not only do the two books display identical themes and style but also the opening words of both books refer to the same person. Luke's Gospel begins:

> Since many have undertaken to set down an orderly account of the events that have been fulfilled among us, just as they were handed on to us by those who from the beginning were eyewitnesses and servants of the word, I too decided, after investigating everything carefully from the first, to write an orderly account for you, most excellent Theophilus, so that you may know the truth concerning the things about which you have been instructed. (Luke 1:1-4)

The author here suggests that he was not an original disciple of Jesus nor an eyewitness of Jesus' ministry but had investigated reports of those who were. His Gospel was intended, at least in part, to inform a certain Theophilus (a new convert?) of what Jesus said and did. This Gospel, then, is not the work of an apostle.

The book of Acts begins:

> In the first book, Theophilus, I wrote about all that Jesus did and taught from the beginning until the day when he was taken up to heaven, after giving instructions through the Holy Spirit to the apostles whom he had chosen. (Acts 1:1-2)

The "first book" certainly is the Gospel of Luke, which ends with a reference to the ascension of Jesus (Luke 24:50-53).

Who was the author? Both books are anonymous, but tradition of the late-2nd-century Christians asserts that he was a man named Luke, the person described in Col. 4:14 as a medical doctor and in Philemon 24 and 2 Tim. 4:11 as a traveling companion of Paul's. It is possible that this man was not a Jew; if so, and if he wrote these two books, he would most probably be the only Gentile author in the New Testament. Who wrote Luke and Acts, however, cannot be known with certainty.

Luke follows Mark's geographical outline, but, instead of a section located on the fringes of Galilee, he has dramatically lengthened the account of Jesus' journey from Galilee to Jerusalem. Luke 9:51–19:27, the "travel narrative" or "special section," corresponds to Mark 10, but it obviously has a good amount of unique material (L) and also draws much from Q.

Among the major themes of Luke are the following:

1. Luke emphasizes the universal mission of Jesus and also that of the early church, which is to be a world religion with no ethnic restrictions. This is suggested already in the words of the aged Simeon at the time of Jesus' birth: "My eyes have seen your salvation, which you have prepared in the presence of all peoples, a light for revelation to the Gentiles and for glory to your people Israel" (Luke 2:30-32). Unlike Matthew, who traces Jesus' ancestry back to Abraham, the father of the Jews, Luke traces it back to Adam, the ancestor of all humankind (3:23-38). In Jesus' first sermon, in Nazareth, he praises a Canaanite woman and a Syrian (4:16-27) and later holds up a Samaritan as a model of moral action (10:29-37). And the risen Jesus announces the preaching of "repentance and forgiveness of sins . . . to all nations, beginning from Jerusalem" (24:47).

2. The Gospel of Luke exhibits a sense of world history and a style reminiscent of some of the Greek historians of antiquity. The author correlates significant events in the life of Jesus and the early church with the names of secular rulers: In Luke 2:1-2 he asserts that, at the time of Jesus' birth, Augustus was emperor of Rome and Quirinius was governor of Syria. He dates the beginning of the preaching of John the Baptist to the "fifteenth year of the reign of Emperor Tiberius [about 29 C.E.], when Pontius Pilate was governor of Judea, and Herod was ruler

of Galilee, and his brother Philip ruler of the region of Ituraea and Trachonitis, and Lysanias ruler of Abilene, during the high priesthood of Annas and Caiaphas" (3:1-3). Luke is the first known Christian who appears to have thought of Christianity as a movement within world history. The author, in the book of Acts, gives time intervals for the periods between Jesus' resurrection and ascension (40 days) and between the ascension and the day of Pentecost (Acts 1:3; 2:1). It is clear that for Luke the end of history was not imminent.

3. Consistent with this sense of history is Luke's apparent desire to demonstrate the political neutrality of the church in relation to Rome. He emphasizes Pilate's pronouncement of Jesus' political innocence ("I have examined him in your presence and have not found this man guilty of any of your charges against him," Luke 23:14; see also 23:4, 20, 22). A Roman soldier who witnesses Jesus' crucifixion says, "Certainly this man was innocent" (Luke 23:47) — not, as in Mark and Matthew, "Truly this man was God's Son." Similarly, in Acts, almost all references to Rome or to Roman officials are positive. Luke's work has a classically apologetic purpose — a defense of the faith before the secular rulers, like that of several Christian writers of the 2nd century.

4. Also in line with Luke's historical interest is his apparent division of history into three large periods: (a) the time of Israel, the time of promise, which runs up to the work of Jesus (or John). "The law and the prophets [that is, the Hebrew Scriptures] were in effect until John came; since then the good news of the kingdom of God is proclaimed, and everyone tries to enter it by force" (Luke 16:16). (b) The ministry of Jesus is the middle of history, the time of fulfillment. (c) The time of the church, for Luke a considerable period, would last until the return of Jesus. In Luke, Jesus corrects his disciples' misunderstanding that the end is imminent (19:11) and warns them that false leaders would tempt them to think that "the time is near" (21:8).

5. Luke associates Jesus with a number of prophetic concerns, including promises of God's special regard for marginalized groups of society: women (7:12, 15; 8:2; 10:38; 23:27; etc.), Samaritans (10:30-37; 17:11-19), repentant sinners (5:1-11; 7:36-50; 15:1-32; 18:9-14; 19:1-10; 22:31-32; etc.), and tax collectors (19:2), among others. The au-

thor, moreover, includes numerous warnings against the temptations and dangers of wealth. Jesus himself emerges as a prophet in Luke 4:24; 7:11-17; 7:39; 13:33; and 24:19.

Jesus in Luke is humane, gracious, inclusive, and redemptive.

The Gospel of John

In many ways the Gospel of John is the enigma of the New Testament. The author's worldview reflects awareness of Greek thought, similar in some respects to the philosophical work of Jewish scholars at Alexandria, but also of Palestinian Jewish traditions as well as peculiar details of the traditions about Jesus. Radical differences between the portrayal of Jesus in this Gospel compared with those in the Synoptic Gospels have puzzled readers for centuries and have raised the question of the relation between theology and history in the Gospel of John.

Little is known with certainty about the origin of this Gospel. Most scholars now speculate that the Gospel of John emerged in final form toward the end of the 1st century C.E., although it might have passed through several earlier editions. Equally little is known about the author, the place of writing, and the original recipients. Christian tradition from the end of the 2nd century was unanimous that the author was the apostle John who, in turn, was thought to be the unnamed "beloved disciple" mentioned several times in the Gospel (John 13:23; 19:26; 20:2; 21:7; 21:20). A postscript to the Gospel (21:24) asserts that the author was, indeed, the "beloved disciple":

> This ["the disciple whom Jesus loved," v. 20] is the disciple who is testifying to these things and has written them, and we know that his testimony is true. (John 21:24)

The document, however, is technically anonymous (the name of the author is not provided in its contents), and even the identity of the beloved disciple remains questionable. John 21:20-23 implies that the beloved disciple was dead when this book was written. Moreover, the differences between John and the Synoptics are so significant that it is difficult to believe that the author of John could have been an eyewitness of the deeds and words of Jesus that he records. This Gospel was apparently not written by an apostle, even though its contents obviously have links with apostolic tradition.

DIFFERENCES FROM THE SYNOPTIC GOSPELS

The challenge of interpreting the Gospel of John can be seen most easily by considering its differences from the Synoptic Gospels, which are considerable.

1. Missing and Unique Materials

John does not explicitly mention several things that are determinative for the picture of Jesus' ministry in the Synoptics, including Jesus' baptism and temptations; Jesus' agony in the Garden of Gethsemane; the words over the bread and wine at the Last Supper; and his dealings with lepers, children, tax collectors, sinners, the poor, and demoniacs. Conversely, John includes a number of narratives and persons who do not appear in the Synoptics, including the wedding at Cana, Nicodemus, the Samaritan woman, Lazarus, and several curious details in the Passion Narrative.

2. The Form of Jesus' Teaching

Aphorisms and parables on matters of everyday life are the two typical forms of Jesus' words in the Synoptics. Neither of these forms occurs in the Gospel of John (the analogy of the Good Shepherd in John 10:1-18 is not an exception). Instead, Jesus' teaching in John typically takes the form of long, abstract discourses or dialogues, some of them based on an incident as a jumping-off point. For example, the discourse on the "bread of life" in 6:25-59 is related to John's narrative of the feeding of the multitude in 6:1-14.

3. The Content of Jesus' Teaching

The unifying theme of Jesus' teaching in the Synoptics is the eschato-logical kingdom of God and the repentance that is required in prepara-tion for its full and final implementation. Neither the verb "to repent" nor the noun "repentance" occurs in the Fourth Gospel, and the expres-sion "kingdom of God" occurs only in 3:3-5. Jesus himself has replaced the kingdom of God as the recurring subject of Jesus' discourses in the Gospel of John: he has come "from above" and will "return to the Fa-ther." Equally striking, the futuristic eschatology of the Synoptics, with its emphasis on the return of the Son of Man, the resurrection of the dead, and the last judgment, has been spiritualized. In this Gospel, Jesus says, "I am the resurrection and the life" (11:25), even though traces of traditional eschatology remain, as in 6:39-40. The author of John re-peatedly suggests that the ultimate judgment occurs in an individual's response to Jesus.

4. The Actions of Jesus

The absence in John of the kinds of people with whom Jesus has deal-ings in the Synoptics is noted above (no. 1). The author appears to have no special concern for the neglected, exploited, or oppressed of society but directs his attention to adults who encounter Jesus' claims. There are miracles, including healings, but with a difference. In John these are called "signs" (see John 2:11, "the first of his signs"; and see below, p. 136), which indicates that the author finds that each one points beyond itself to the truth Jesus expresses in his discourses. They are, in short, opportunities for the beginning of faith. There are in John only seven "signs," given to a "world" that is deaf (ch. 8), blind (ch. 9), ignorant (ch. 7), and dying (ch. 11). Whether the author considered Jesus' cruci-fixion as the final and greatest of his "signs" is not clear.

5. The Scene of Jesus' Activity

Matthew and Luke generally follow Mark's outline, which locates Jesus' activity in a rather small area near the northwest part of the Sea of Galilee, followed by trips to Phoenicia and the area near Mount Hermon, and then a journey to Jerusalem, where Jesus was crucified a few days after his arrival. In John the scene has shifted radically to Jerusalem — and particularly the temple area during festival periods. (Jesus is in Galilee in the Fourth Gospel from 1:43 to 2:13; 4:43 to 5:1; 6:1 to 7:10; and, a narrative of resurrection appearances in ch. 21.) Although the author knows that Nazareth was Jesus' hometown ("Can anything good come out of Nazareth?" John 1:46), a comparison of Mark with John shows that John considered Jesus' true home to be elsewhere:

> He . . . came to his hometown. . . . On the sabbath he began to teach in the synagogue, and many who heard him were astounded. They said, "Where did this man get all this? . . . Is not this the carpenter, the son of Mary and brother of James and Joses and Judas and Simon, and are not his sisters here with us?" And they took offense at him. Then Jesus said to them, "Prophets are not without honor, except in their hometown, and among their own kin, and in their own house." . . . And he was amazed at their unbelief. (Mark 6:1-6)

> When the two days were over, he went from that place [Samaria] to Galilee (for Jesus himself had testified that a prophet has no honor in the prophet's own country). When he came to Galilee, the Galileans welcomed him, since they had seen all that he had done in Jerusalem at the festival. . . . (John 4:43-45)

In John, Jesus' "home" is Jerusalem, but ultimately his home is "from above." This explains the frequency of the question that lies behind so many passages in the Fourth Gospel, namely, where Jesus comes from. John 7:25-29 is typical:

> Now some of the people of Jerusalem were saying, "Is not this the man whom they are trying to kill? And here he is, speaking openly,

but they say nothing to him! Can it be that the authorities really know that this is the Messiah? Yet we know where this man is from; but when the Messiah comes, no one will know where he is from." Then Jesus cried out as he was teaching in the temple, "You know me, and you know where I am from. I have not come on my own. But the one who sent me is true, and you do not know him. I know him, because I am from him, and he sent me."

6. Irony and Misunderstanding

As in the Synoptics, those whom Jesus encounters in John often fail to grasp his point because of their general obtuseness. In John the cause most often is that Jesus uses ordinary terms — water, bread, birth, blindness — to speak of his origin with God, his "descent" to this world, and his impending "return" to the Father. "How can anyone be born after having grown old?" (3:4). "Sir, you have no bucket, and the well is deep. Where do you get that living water?" (4:11). "How can this man give us his flesh to eat?" (6:52). "I know that he [Martha's brother, Lazarus] will rise again in the resurrection on the last day" (11:24).

7. John's Church and "the Jews"

The Synoptic Gospels often depict Jesus in a polemical situation with a variety of Jewish leaders: scribes, Pharisees, Sadducees, Herodians, and others. The distinctive aspects of the belief and concerns of each group are usually recognized, and Jesus clearly speaks as a Jew and, most often, to Jews. In John, the breach between Jews and Christians is nearing completeness, with polemics sharpened to vituperation. This fact is announced already in the prologue: "He came to what was his own, and his own people did not accept him" (John 1:11).

One of the most explicit examples of the breach is John 8:31-59, a conversation between Jesus and "the Jews who had believed in him" (8:31). "The Jews" accuse Jesus of illegitimacy (8:41) and of being a Samaritan (8:48) and a demoniac (8:48). Jesus retorts that their father is the devil (8:44) and labels them slaves of sin (8:34), liars, and murderers

(8:44). Such language — so catastrophic in its aftermath — suggests the dynamics of a small cult in relation to the mother religion.

A possible indication of the final date of writing of the Gospel of John is the fact that the Pharisees were the authorities of Judaism as it was known to the author in the late 1st century. Although there are references to "priests and Levites" (1:19), "scribes" (8:3), and "chief priests" (11:47, 57; 18:3), these are mentioned alongside of the Pharisees. (It was the Pharisees who saved Judaism after the destruction of the Roman War, and the author of the Fourth Gospel might have been aware of the reconstruction that was beginning at Jamnia toward the end of the 1st century.) Pharisees send priests and Levites to check on the Baptist (1:24; see 4:1); the Pharisee Nicodemus is "a leader of the Jews" (3:1; 19:39); Pharisees send temple police to arrest Jesus already in chapter 7 (vv. 32-48); they challenge Jesus' authority (8:13); criticize Jesus' healing of the blind man (9:13-40); continue to plot Jesus' death (11:46-57); exclude from the synagogues those who believed in Jesus (12:19, 42); and are involved in Jesus' arrest (18:3).

The Sadducees, by contrast, are mentioned nowhere in the Gospel of John.

8. Jesus in John

Jesus in the Synoptic Gospels has been viewed by scholars today in a variety of categories of 1st-century Judaism, but the most compelling picture is that of eschatological prophet. The Synoptics already show the influence of Christian veneration of Jesus as the divine Son of God who has unique authority and glory, but they retain the human features of Jesus, describing his everyday interactions with real persons of the time, his temptations, emotions, human agony, and the limitation of his knowledge. By contrast, in John Jesus from the start is aware of his divine origin with the Father, the need for him to be "glorified" and "lifted up" in his crucifixion, and his impending "return to the Father." The traditional doctrine of the incarnation is laid out in this Gospel and constitutes the essential theme of Jesus' teaching there.

9. Literary Unity

The Synoptics, in spite of evidence of significant editorial work on sources, and with the exception of the Passion Narrative, generally consist of individual pericopes assembled in a loose framework. In most cases, a few narratives or sayings could be deleted without disturbing the flow or disrupting the style, and a specific text can often be fruitfully examined by itself. The Gospel of John is much more a literary unity. A distinctive Greek style and vocabulary — and an idiomatic theology — permeate the entire work, including both the narratives and the discourses of Jesus. Despite this, there is often a subtle relationship between John and the Synoptics; the author of John in significant ways sometimes appears to offer a reinterpretation of Synoptic themes and passages.

Whether John knew any of the Synoptics is a matter of intense debate, and speculation about the origin of the unique aspects of his Gospel has spawned a host of scholarly tomes. From the time that Clement of Alexandria (approximately 150-203 C.E.) asserted that John, in contrast to Matthew, Mark, and Luke, wrote "a spiritual Gospel," it has been customary to refer to the author as "John the divine" (John the theologian) and to recognize his Gospel as a theological work. Debate over the balance in John between history and theology has continued to the present.

STRUCTURE

The Gospel of John has a well-defined structure:

Prologue (1:1-18) and Beginnings (1:19-51)

The main theme of the Gospel of John is announced toward the end of the prologue: "And the Word [Greek: *logos*] became flesh and lived among us . . ." (1:14). The history of the word *logos* in Greek and Jewish tradition enabled John to explain (1) how a transcendent God could have dealings with an alienated world and (2) how monotheism could — in some sense — be maintained along with the divinity of Jesus.

Jesus' Public Ministry, the "Book of Signs" (Chapters 2–12)

Jesus' public actions in John are called "signs" (2:11, 18, 23; 3:2; 4:54; 6:2; 7:31; 9:16; 10:41; 11:47; 12:18, 37; 20:30), by which the author suggests that they have symbolic meaning. The themes of the first section are new wine (2:1-11), new temple (2:13-22), new birth (3:1-10), and new worship (4:1-30).

Jesus' Private Instruction of the Disciples, the "Farewell Discourses" and the "High Priestly Prayer" (Chapters 13–17)

John creates a structural separation between Jesus' public teaching and his private instruction of the disciples, a distinction that is incipient already in the Synoptics (see Mark 4:33-34). The long monologues of John 13:31–16:33, contrary to some first impressions, are carefully constructed and subtly related to themes found in the private instruction of the disciples by Jesus in the Synoptic Gospels. Examples are (1) precepts, warnings, and promises to the disciples, (2) predictions of the death and resurrection of Jesus, and (3) eschatological predictions. But each of these is carried out in distinctly Johannine terminology.

The Passion and Resurrection (Chapters 18–20)

The account of Jesus' death and resurrection in John differs in several respects from the narrative in the Synoptics.

1. Chronology: Mark (see 14:12), followed by Matthew and Luke, presupposes that the Last Supper was the Passover meal that year and that Jesus was crucified on the day of Passover. According to John 13:1; 19:14, 31, the Passover that year began Friday evening, so that Jesus was crucified at the very time that the lambs were being slaughtered for the meal. No one has yet convincingly harmonized these conflicting texts.

2. John does not mention the following Synoptic details: supernatu-

ral phenomena (darkening of the sun, splitting of the temple curtain, earthquakes, apparitions of dead saints, the healing of the servant's ear), Jesus praying in Gethsemane, the charge of blasphemy (or any other specific charge) against Jesus at the Jewish hearing, Simon of Cyrene carrying Jesus' cross, the mocking and reviling of Jesus on the cross, and the words uttered by Jesus from the cross, most notably the cry of dereliction, "My God, my God, why have you forsaken me?"

3. Unique aspects of John's Passion Narrative include:

- The emphasis of the "glorification" of Jesus in his death (see already 17:1)
- The Jews' insistence that Pilate pass the sentence (19:12)
- The "fulfillment" of several Old Testament passages (John 19:28, 37)
- The episode of Jesus' mother and the "disciple whom he loved" (19:26-27)
- The last cry of Jesus, "It is finished," which means that his mission from God has been accomplished (19:30)
- The mention that water and blood flowed from the body of Jesus (19:34)
- The assertion that the body of Jesus had been anointed for burial (19:38-40)

All of these curious differences relate to the distinctive aim of the author, consistent with what had been articulated in the preceding chapters.

4. Also in John's account of Jesus' resurrection, there are several unique features:

- Not only the women but also Peter and the disciple "whom Jesus loved" witnessed the empty tomb, including the position of the grave clothes (20:2-10).
- The risen Jesus "breathed on" his disciples and said, "Receive the Holy Spirit" (20:22). This appears to be John's equivalent of Luke's story of Pentecost (Acts 2).
- The scene of Jesus and doubting Thomas (20:24-29) is unique to

John's Gospel. After he witnessed the marks of the crucifixion on Jesus' body, Thomas makes what the author undoubtedly considered the most appropriate confession of faith, "My Lord and my God!" (20:28).

- John's account of appearances of the risen Jesus in Galilee (John 21) has no real parallels in the Synoptics (Matt. 28:16-20 is quite different in content).

Appendix: Other Appearances of the Risen Jesus (Chapter 21)

John 20:30-31 has the appearance of a conclusion to this Gospel; there the author informs us why he wrote. Some scholars, therefore, think that chapter 21 is an appendix by a different person, an appendix added by the same author at a later time, or that the author intended the book to stand as we have it.

- Verses 24-25 present a problem in that they imply that the "beloved disciple," mentioned five times earlier in the Gospel, is the author.
- Verse 24, "This is the disciple who is testifying to these things and has written them, and we know that his testimony is true," appears to be an explanation of 19:35, where, after mentioning that blood and water came from Jesus' crucified body, the author writes, "He who saw this has testified so that you also may believe. His testimony is true, and he knows that he tells the truth." John 21:24, then, would be later than 19:35.
- Although Jerusalem — and especially the temple — is the central location of Jesus' activity in the Gospel of John, the appearances in chapter 21 take place in Galilee.
- In the body of the book, the emphasis is on the past coming of Jesus — his earthly ministry. Jesus there predicted that the Holy Spirit would function as the guide of the believers after Jesus' death. In chapter 21, however, the more traditional emphasis is found: Jesus will return in the future (v. 23).

• John 21 narrates the rehabilitation of Peter (21:15-17) after his denial of Jesus during the trial (18:25-27).

The Gospel of John, with its strange combination of detailed asides and abstract theology, will continue to fascinate and puzzle readers for years to come. The author was a person of subtle mind who represents a closed-in group of believers under pressure.

Reading the Gospels

As a distinctive if not unique literary form, the Gospels of the New Testament present abundant challenges to today's reader. The combination of history and proclamation in the Gospels can be almost impossible to disentangle, the differences between them bewildering, and their thought-world and social context alien to 21st-century persons. Nonetheless, a rapid reading of the Gospel of Mark can leave in the reader's mind the impression of strong drama and immediacy as well as a general sense of the impression Jesus' activity left on his followers. A reading of Matthew and Luke provides a fuller account of Jesus' teaching than is found in Mark, while the Gospel of John — the most difficult of the four by any account — is an attempt to put the figure of Jesus in the context both of the abstract cosmology of the time and also of disputes between Christians and other Jews. The distinctiveness of the New Testament Gospels can be sensed by a reading of the most intriguing of the extrabiblical Gospels, the Gospel of Thomas, and then perhaps the pagan *Life of Apollonius,* by Philostratus.

A first-time thoughtful reader of the Gospels is well advised to avoid thinking that these documents are straightforward historical reports or biographies in the modern sense. By their own statements (see Mark 1:1; John 20:31) they are attempts to convince the reader of the divine, unique ordination of Jesus as teacher and eschatological deliverer. Many passages in the Gospels draw on memories of Jesus' words and deeds to deal with conflicts between Jesus' followers and members of the synagogues or with disputes and practices within the new congregations.

Other texts are concerned to show that Jesus' appearance and fate were foretold in the Old Testament or that his resurrection was an exaltation by God after his ignominious death. The question whether a given text more closely reflects the activity and teaching of Jesus or that of the subsequent Christian communities is perhaps the most difficult of all when reading the Gospels. There is some comfort, however, in knowing that this is a matter of ongoing debate among scholars and ordinary readers worldwide.

IO

Conclusion: Making Sense of the Bible

The Bible can begin to make sense when we appreciate the variety of literature it contains and the spectrum of interests on the part of the individuals and groups that produced it. I hope that this book has afforded you a glimpse of the broad range of writing in the Bible and also the kind of content you can expect to find in each of its major literary types. With the Bible, as with so many other subjects that have attracted the scrutiny of academicians for generations, the more we delve into the matter the more fascinating it becomes.

At the same time, however, reading the Bible with an ear to what the authors were saying and how they said it does not necessarily make any easier the problem of applying its teachings or values to life today. The opposite could well be the case. Many persons who look to the Bible for guidance in life focus on one strand within it, or perhaps a selection of texts without regard to the context. Although such reading might have some merit, there is more to be said for grasping the shape of the whole, becoming self-aware of our own choices and selections among the parts of the Bible.

The Bible will no doubt continue to be a central resource in the development of spirituality for many. Through the human words, written by so many different kinds of persons and reflecting various perspectives, readers might find themselves gripped by unexpected insights that elevate consciousness and transcend both author and reader. Perhaps at such serendipitous moments the ancient writings can *become* the word of God for the reader. Before this can happen in a responsible way, however, it is necessary for us to appreciate the concrete nature of both text and ancient author. What follows from that cannot be predicted.

Reading with understanding is an art that necessarily involves a reciprocal relationship between reader and text. The collection of ancient literature that we call the Bible confronts the reader with special challenges that result from vastly different social structures, worldviews, languages, and even values. With a little effort it is nonetheless possible to make sense of the Bible if we keep in mind some simple principles:

1. *Cultivate curiosity.* In my career as a college teacher I noticed that those students who developed interests beyond their specific vocational goals were not only most likely to succeed in the classroom and after graduation but also to have fuller and more productive lives. Whatever perspective you bring to the reading of the Bible, chances are that the growth you experience from reading these ancient texts will not only quicken your mind but also — sooner or later — prove to be more relevant to your life than you expected. Learning requires curiosity.

2. *Appreciate diversity.* The above chapters suggest the range of basic forms of literature in the Bible. This literary variety reflects also the variety of social groups from which it stems: nomadic tribes (for example, some narratives in Genesis 12-50), priests (including the law codes and much of the editing of narrative material), the royal court (annals in 1-2 Kings; some Psalms), shepherds and farmers (like Amos), sages (wisdom writers), itinerant preachers (the Gospel writers), and others. The literature also reflects competing ideologies of the various social groups, from conservative virtues to revolutionary passion.

3. *Ask the big questions.* What kind of person wrote this text and why? What kind of thought-world had the author constructed? What did the author consider to be of prime importance? What made life worth living for him or her?

4. *Become self-aware in your dialogue with the text.* The dynamics of

reading are exceedingly complex and have been subjected to close scrutiny by whole contingents of scholars. Making sense of the Bible — understanding the text — involves an awareness of the interplay between your mental activity in reading and the text before you. What are the interests and preconceptions that drove you to the text in the first place? Identify the points of contact between your interests and the interests you perceive on the part of the author. Allow your preconceptions to be challenged. In other words, be prepared to grow.

Forms of Ancient Hebrew Poetry

One-third of the Old Testament and parts of the New Testament are poetic in form. This includes the Psalms, most of the wisdom literature, and much of the prophetic books. Only seven Old Testament books have no poetic lines (Leviticus, Ruth, Esther, Ezra-Nehemiah, Haggai, and Malachi). Moreover, much of the earliest literature that came to be included in the Old Testament is poetic: the Song of Lamech (Gen. 4:23-24), the Song of Miriam (Exod. 15:21), the Song of the Ark (Num. 10:35-36), the Book of Jashar (Josh. 10:12-13; 2 Sam. 1:18), the Book of the Wars of YHWH (Num. 21:14-15), the Song of Deborah (Judg. 5), and others.

For centuries the formal characteristics of Hebrew poetry had been forgotten and unobserved. Although in the Hebrew manuscripts of the Old Testament three books — the Psalms, Proverbs, and Job — are arranged in poetic form, the Greek and Latin manuscripts paid no attention at all to the differences between prose and poetry. Among English translations, the Revised Standard Version (1952) was the first to make this distinction consistently. The reading of prose and poetry without distinguishing between them often led to eccentric and fanciful interpretations of the text. For example, it is possible that in the account of Jesus' entry into Jerusalem in Matt. 21:5 there is a misreading or overly literal interpretation of the quotation from Zech. 9:9:

A1   Lo, your king comes to you;
   A2   triumphant and victorious is he,
B1   humble and riding on a donkey,
   B2   on a colt, the foal of a donkey.

Mark 11:7 and Luke 19:30-35 mention only one animal, but Matthew thinks there were two, possibly because of the synonymous parallelism of the two B stichs in Zech. 9:9.

Robert Lowth of Oxford, England, made a lasting contribution to biblical studies in 1753 with the publication of *Lectures on the Sacred Poetry of the Hebrews,* which was followed in 1787 by a translation of the book of Isaiah. Lowth identified the essential feature of ancient Hebrew poetry, "parallelism of members," the placing of two or three lines in parallel position with each other, and he tried to classify the various types of parallelism used in the poetry of the Old Testament. Among the most common types are:

Internal Parallelism

Internal parallelism involves two or three lines within one strophe. Typical is Ps. 24:1-4:

A1   The earth is YHWH's and all that is in it,
   A2   the world, and those who live in it;
B1   for he has founded it on the seas,
   B2   and established it on the rivers.
C1   Who shall ascend the hill of YHWH?
   C2   And who shall stand in his holy place?
D1   Those who have clean hands and pure hearts,
   D2   who do not lift up their souls to what is false,
   D3   and do not swear deceitfully.

Each line can be called a "stich" or "stichos" (from the Greek), and each set of parallels a "distich" (if there are two stichs) or "tristich" (if three).

In *synonymous parallelism* the same thought is conveyed in successive stichs, as in Psalm 24; there is no change of meaning or purpose from A1 to A2, although the second line can echo the first completely or only in part.

Antithetic parallelism displays an opposition or contrast of thought, which was especially fitting for the contrasts of proverbs:

A1 The poor are disliked even by their neighbors,
   A2 but the rich have many friends.   (Prov. 14:20)

A1 For YHWH watches over the way of the righteous,
   A2 but the way of the wicked will perish.   (Ps. 1:6)

In *synthetic parallelism* the second stich advances the thought of the first, a formal pattern that involves rhythm and meter:

A1 The fool says in his heart,
   A2 "There is no God."
B1 They are corrupt, they do abominable deeds;
   B2 there is none that does good.
C1 YHWH looks down from heaven
   C2 upon the children of men
D1 to see if there are any that act wisely,
   D2 that seek after God. (Ps. 14:1-2, RSV)

The A and C stichs here are in synthetic parallelism, while B and D are synonymous.

There are other kinds of *miscellaneous* internal parallelism, including

• similes and metaphors:

A1 Like the partridge hatching what it did not lay,
   A2 so are all who amass wealth unjustly. . . .   (Jer. 17:11)

- Stairlike or "climactic" parallelism, with a partial repetition combined with an advance (recapitulation plus extension):

A1   Ascribe to YHWH, O heavenly beings,
    A2   ascribe to YHWH glory and strength.
B1   Ascribe to YHWH the glory of his name;
    B2   Worship YHWH in holy splendor.   (Ps. 29:1)

- Inverted parallelism:

A1   Ephraim shall not be jealous of Judah,
    A2   and Judah shall not be hostile towards Ephraim.
                (Isa. 11:13)

External Parallelism

External parallelism is a correspondence between or among two or more distichs or tristichs. A simple example of four stichs is Isa. 1:10:

A1   Hear the word of YHWH,
    A2   you rulers of Sodom!
B1   Listen to the teaching of our God,
    B2   you people of Gomorrah!

The two A stichs are in synonymous parallel position to the B stichs.
    Other techniques of Hebrew poetry can most often be seen only in the original Hebrew text:

- meter (the rhythm of accented syllables)
- alliteration (similar sounds in the beginning of the words)
- assonance (similar sounds in the vowels of the words)
- paronomasia or puns, found especially in the poetry of the prophets
- acrostic (the first letters of stichs follow the sequence of the Hebrew alphabet)
- onomatopoeia (the aping of actual sound in the sound of the words)

Because most English translations of the Bible of the past several decades distinguish between prose and poetry in the way the text is laid out on the page, readers today should have little difficulty in identifying a specific text as poetry — or at least in observing the translators' decision on the matter.

APPENDIX B

Major Literary Types and Selected in Biblical References

Genesis: Quasi-historical narratives	36-37
Exodus: Quasi-historical narratives, law codes	37-38, 66-68
Leviticus: Law codes	69-70
Numbers: Censuses, quasi-historical narratives, laws	39, 70
Deuteronomy: Law codes	39, 68-69
Joshua: Quasi-historical narratives, geographical data	40
Judges: Quasi-historical narratives (tribal sagas)	40-41
Ruth: Narrative (short story)	
1-2 Samuel: Historical and quasi-historical narratives	41-42, 55
1-2 Kings: Historical and quasi-historical narratives	11-12, 42-44, 52-56
1-2 Chronicles: Genealogies, quasi-historical narratives	42
Ezra: Historical and quasi-historical narratives	45-46, 81
Nehemiah: Historical and quasi-historical narratives	45-46
Job: Wisdom literature (with narrative prologue and epilogue)	16-21
Psalms: Worship materials	26-30
Proverbs: Wisdom literature	14-16
Ecclesiastes: Wisdom literature	21-23
Song of Solomon: Love poetry	
Isaiah: Prophecy	57-59, 62-64
Jeremiah: Prophecy	44, 59-62, 82
Lamentations: National lament (liturgical literature)	27

Ezekiel: Prophecy   44
Daniel: Apocalypse   52, 74-77
Hosea: Prophecy
Joel: National lament (liturgical literature)   27
Amos: Prophecy   56-57
Obadiah: Prophecy
Jonah: Narrative (short story)
Micah: Prophecy
Nahum: Prophecy
Habakkuk: Prophecy   26
Zephaniah: Prophecy
Haggai: Prophecy
Zechariah: Prophecy and apocalyptic literature
Malachi: Prophecy
Matthew: Gospel   31-32, 70-71, 95-96, 123-26
Mark: Gospel   94, 98-123
Luke: Gospel   95-96, 126-29
John: Gospel   129-39
Acts: Historical and quasi-historical narratives   30, 47-51
Romans: Letter   87-89
1-2 Corinthians: Letters   84-87
Galatians: Letter   89-90
Ephesians: Letter   30
Philippians: Letter   31-32
Colossians: Letter   31
1-2 Thessalonians: Letters   83
1-2 Timothy: General Letters   30, 90
Titus: General Letter   30, 90
Philemon: Letter   48
Hebrews: Written sermon or general letter   90
James: Wisdom literature   23-24
1-2 Peter: General Letters   7, 90
1-3 John: General Letters   80, 90
Jude: General Letter   80, 90
Revelation: Apocalypse   30, 77-79
1 Maccabbes: Historical and quasi-historical narratives   46-47

Suggestions for Further Reading

From introductions to technical studies, the plethora of books on the Bible can be off-putting and bewildering. The list below is one way to get into more technical aspects of issues raised in this book.

Introduction to the Bible

Harris, Stephen L. *Understanding the Bible.* 5th ed. Mountain View, Ca-
    lif.: Mayfield, 2000. An expanded edition of an accessible,
    nonsectarian introduction, this book includes methods of interpreta-
    tion, biblical history from Sumer to the Romans, and comments
    from a historical-critical perspective on all books of the Bible.

Methods of Bible Study

Aageson, James W. *In the Beginning: Critical Concepts for the Study of the
    Bible.* Boulder: Westview, 2000. An introduction for the nonspecial-
    ist to the methods and assumptions of critical biblical studies, em-
    phasizing historical-critical methods.
McKenzie, Steven L., and Stephen R. Haynes, eds. *To Each Its Own
    Meaning: An Introduction to Biblical Criticisms and Their Application.*
    Louisville: Westminster John Knox, 1993. Thirteen scholars describe
    their preferred methods of interpreting the Bible. The chapters are ar-

ranged according to methods labeled (1) traditional, (2) expanding the traditional, and (3) countering the traditional.

Literary Forms of the Bible

Dormeyer, Detlev. *The New Testament among the Writings of Antiquity.* Biblical Seminar 55. Sheffield: Sheffield Academic, 1998. A comparison of literary forms in the New Testament with their use in ancient Greco-Roman and Jewish literature.

Wisdom Literature

Bergant, Dianne. *Israel's Wisdom Literature.* Minneapolis: Fortress, 1997. An accessible approach from a liberation perspective.

Blenkinsopp, Joseph. *Sage, Priest, Prophet: Religious and Intellectual Leadership in Ancient Israel.* Library of Ancient Israel. Louisville: Westminster John Knox, 1995. Chapter 1, "The Sage," has helpful information on the background and nature of wisdom literature.

Jamieson-Drake, David W. *Scribes and Schools in Monarchic Judah: A Socio-Archaeological Approach.* JSOT Supplement 109. Sheffield: Almond, 1991. This technical work maintains that scribal schools flourished in the 8th and 7th centuries B.C.E. in connection with centralized administration, increasing commerce, and growing social stratification.

The Psalms

Brueggemann, Walter. *Spirituality of the Psalms.* Minneapolis: Fortress, 2001. Centers on the contemporary thrust of three categories: psalms of orientation, psalms of disorientation, and psalms of new orientation.

Holladay, William L. *The Psalms through Three Thousand Years: Prayerbook of a Cloud of Witnesses.* Minneapolis: Fortress, 1993. Delightful and stimulating account of the influence of the Psalms in subsequent history.

Miller, Patrick D. *They Cried to the Lord: The Form and Theology of Biblical Prayer.* Minneapolis: Fortress, 1994. A comprehensive, readable analysis.

Biblical Narratives

Fokkelman, Jan P. *Reading Biblical Narrative: An Introductory Guide.* Louisville: Westminster John Knox, 1999. How to get beyond one's own presuppositions in reading biblical texts. Centers on Old Testament narratives of Israel's patriarchs, judges, and kings, with one chapter on New Testament narratives.

Powell, Mark Allan. *What Is Narrative Criticism?* Guides to Biblical Scholarship. Minneapolis: Fortress, 1990.

Trible, Phyllis. *Texts of Terror: Literary-Feminist Readings of Biblical Narrative.* Overtures to Biblical Theology 13. Philadelphia: Fortress, 1984. A classic example of observing the subtleties of Old Testament narratives.

Prophetic Literature

Brueggemann, Walter. *The Prophetic Imagination.* Rev. ed. Minneapolis: Fortress, 2001. Traces the prophetic vision from Moses to Jesus.

Heschel, Abraham Joshua. *The Prophets: An Introduction.* New York: Harper & Row, 1962. Repr. Peabody, Mass.: Prince, 1999. Explores the interior understanding of the prophets in sequence and also thematically.

Rad, Gerhard von. *The Message of the Prophets.* New York: Harper & Row, 1972. The nature of Hebrew prophecy and the message of the individual prophets.

Law Codes

Blenkinsopp, Joseph. *Wisdom and Law in the Old Testament.* Rev. ed. Oxford: Oxford University Press, 1995. Note especially chapter 4, "The Growth of Israel's Legal Tradition."

Crüsemann, Frank. *The Torah: Theology and Social History of Old Testament Law.* Minneapolis: Fortress, 1996. A technical account of the origin and development of the law codes of the Old Testament from the beginning to the process of canonization.

Watts, James W. *Reading Law: The Rhetorical Shaping of the Pentateuch.* Biblical Seminar 59. Sheffield: Sheffield Academic, 1999. The relation of lists of laws to narratives in the Pentateuch; a rhetorical-critical perspective.

Apocalyptic Literature

Russell, D. S. *Divine Disclosure: An Introduction to Jewish Apocalyptic.* Philadelphia: Fortress, 1978. A nontechnical, balanced overview.

Letters

Doty, William G. *Letters in Primitive Christianity.* Guides to Biblical Scholarship. Philadelphia: Fortress, 1973.
See also Dormeyer, *The New Testament.*

Gospels

Powell, Mark Allan. *Fortress Introduction to the Gospels.* Minneapolis: Fortress, 1998. A readable account of the origin and themes of the New Testament Gospels.

Rhoads, David, Joanna Dewey, and Donald Michie. *Mark as Story: An Introduction to the Narrative of a Gospel.* 2nd ed. Minneapolis: Fortress, 1999. Mark from the perspective of narrative criticism. Note especially pp. 147-50, "Reading as Dialogue: The Ethics of Reading."
See also Dormeyer, *The New Testament.*

The Forms of Ancient Hebrew Poetry

Anderson, George W. "Characteristics of Hebrew Poetry." In *The New Oxford Annotated Bible with the Apocryphal/Deuterocanonical Books,* ed. Bruce M. Metzger and Roland E. Murphy. New York: Oxford University Press, 1991. Pp. 392-97. An accessible introduction with examples.

Petersen, David L., and Kent Harold Richards. *Interpreting Hebrew Poetry.* Guides to Biblical Scholarship. Minneapolis: Fortress, 1992.

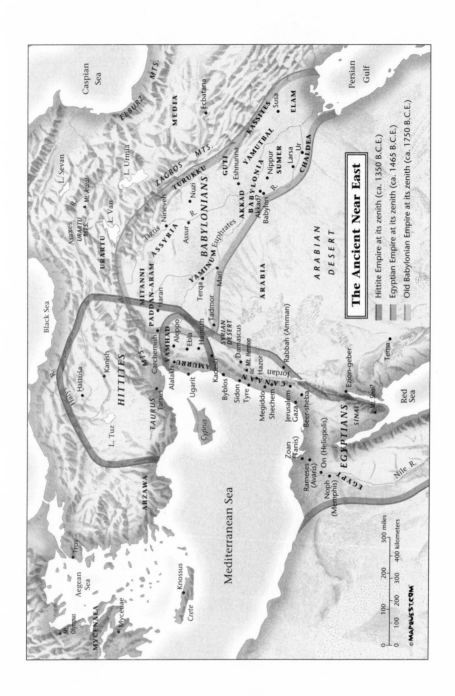

The Ancient Near East

Hittite Empire at its zenith (ca. 1350 B.C.E.)
Egyptian Empire at its zenith (ca. 1465 B.C.E.)
Old Babylonian Empire at its zenith (ca. 1750 B.C.E.)

Caspian Sea

Persian Gulf

ELBURZ MTS.

MEDIA

Ecbatana

L. Sevan

L. Urmia

ZAGROS MTS.

TURUKKU

KASSITES

ELAM

Araxes R.

Mt. Ararat

URARTU MTS.

L. Van

YAMUTBAL

Susa

GUTI

NIPPUR

CHALDEA

Tigris

Nineveh

Nuzi

BABYLONIA

Ur

Assur

R.

Eshnunna

Larsa

SUMER

YAMINUM

ASSYRIA

AKKAD

BABYLON

R.

Akkad?

Babylon

Euphrates

MITANNI

Haran

Terqa

Mari

PADDAN-ARAM

Tadmor

ARABIAN DESERT

Black Sea

Halys R.

Hattuša

Kanish

Carchemish

YAMHAD

Aleppo

Ebla

Hamath

SYRIAN DESERT

ARABIA

HITTITES

TAURUS MTS.

Tarsus

Alalakh

AMURRU

Kadesh

Ugarit

Damascus

Mt. Hermon

Rabbah (Amman)

ARZAWA

L. Tuz

Byblos

Sidon

Tyre

Hazor

Jordan R.

Ezion-geber

Tema

Troy

Cyprus

Megiddo

Shechem

Jerusalem

Beer-sheba

SINAI

Mt. Sinai?

Red Sea

MYCENAEA

Mycenae

Mt. Olympus

Aegean Sea

Knossos

Crete

Mediterranean Sea

Zoan (Tanis)

On (Heliopolis)

Rameses (Avaris)

Noph (Memphis)

EGYPT

EGYPTIANS

Nile R.

0   100   200   300 miles
0   100   200   300   400 kilometers

©MAPQUEST.COM

The Divided Monarchy: Israel and Judah

Beirut

PHOENICIA

Sidon

Litani R.

Abana R.

Damascus

Mt. Hermon

Pharpar R.

Tyre

ARAM

Dan

Kedesh

J. Jarmuk

Hazor

Acco

Sea of
Galilee

Mediterranean
Sea

Mt. Carmel

Mt.
Tabor

Ashtaroth

Kishon

Yarmuk R.

Edrei

Megiddo

Mt. Moreh

Beth-shan

Ramoth-gilead

Taanach

R.

Mt.
Gilboa

Ibleam

Jordan R.

Jabesh-gilead?

Tirzah

Samaria

Mt. Ebal

Succoth?

Penuel?

Mahanaim?

Mt. Gerizim

Shechem

Jabbok R.

Yarkon R.

Joppa

Aphek

Shiloh

ISRAEL

Rabbah (Amman)

Bethel

Jericho

AMMON

Gezer

Ashdod

Aijalon

Jerusalem

Mt. Nebo

Heshbon

Gath

Bethlehem

Medeba

Ashkelon

Mareshah

Gaza

Hebron

Dibon

Gerar

Dead
Sea

Arnon R.

Raphia

JUDAH

Besor Br.

Beer-sheba

MOAB

Kir-hareseth

PHILISTIA

Zered Br.

WILDERNESS

W. el-Aris

Region
periodically
contested
by Judah
and Edom

Bozrah

Kadesh-
barnea

EDOM

0   10   20   30   40 miles

0 10 20 30 40 kilometers

WILDERNESS

© MAPQUEST.COM

Palestine in the
1st Century CE

Extent of Herod's kingdom
■ Herodian fortress city
○ Decapolis city (time of Herod)
• Other city

ABILENE

Abila

Sidon

ITUREA

Abana R.

Damascus

SYRIA

Mt. Hermon

Pharpar R.

Leontes R.

PHOENICIA

Tyre

Caesarea Philippi

TRACHONITIS

Raphana

L. Huleh

Hazor

I. Jarmuk

GALILEE

Chorazin

GAULANITI

TETRARCHY
OF PHILIP

Ptolemais
(Acco)

Capernaum

Bethsaida

Gennesaret

Gergesa

Mt. Carmel

Kishon R.

Cana

Magdala

Sea
of Galilee

Hippos

BATANEA

Sepphoris

Tiberias

Mt. Tabor

Yarmuk R.

AURANITIS

Nazareth

Nain

Gadara

Abila

Mediterranean
Sea

Dor

Megiddo

Scythopolis

Pella

Caesarea
(Strato's Tower)

Dion

DECAPOLIS

SAMARIA

Salim

Sebaste
(Samaria)

Mt. Ebal

Gerasa

Jordan R.

Sychar

Amathus

Mt. Gerizim

Jabbok R.

Me-Jarkon R.

Antipatris
(Aphek)

Alexandrium

PEREA

Joppa

Philadelphia
(Amman)

(SEMI-INDEPENDENT
MUNICIPALITY)

Cyprus

Jericho

Esbus (Heshbon)

Jamnia

Emmaus

Mt. Olivet

Azotus
(Ashdod)

Jerusalem

Bethany

Bethany
beyond Jordan

Medeba

Bethlehem

Hyrcania

Ashkelon

JUDEA

Herodium

Machaerus

Hebron

Adora

Gaza

Dead
Sea

Arnon R.

Raphia

Besor Br.

IDUMEA

Masada

Arad

NABATEA

Beer-sheba

Malatha

Zered Br.

N

0   10   20   30 Miles
0   10   20   30 Kilometers

©MAPQUEST.COM

158

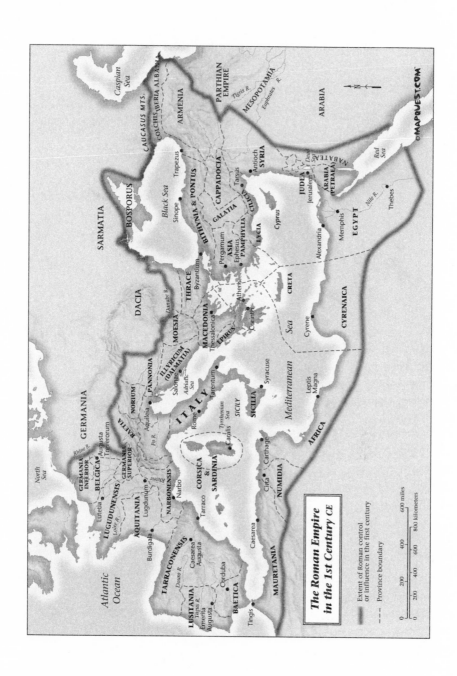

**The Roman Empire
in the 1st Century CE**

— Extent of Roman control
or influence in the first century

- - - Province boundary

0   200   400   600 miles
0   200   400   600   800 kilometers

159

Index

(For biblical references see Appendix B.)

Ahab, 43
Ahaz, 58
Alexander the Great, 46
Amos, 56-57
Anti-Judaism in John, 133-34
Antiochus IV "Epiphanes," 46-47, 75
Apocalyptic literature, 73-79, 112-13
Apocrypha, 6, 46
Apollonius, 92, 139
Apollos, 84

Baalism (Canaanite religion), 41, 55
Baruch, 60
Beloved disciple, 129

Canon, 5
Conquest, 40
Cornelius, 49
Covenant Code, 68
Cyrus, 45, 62-63

David, 26, 42
Deuteronomic history, 39

Elijah, 55-56, 109

Ezra, 45-46

Form criticism, 97

Glossolalia, 86
God, names and terms for, 6, 36-37

Hebrew Bible, 4, 5
Hebrew poetry, ancient, 144-48
Herod "the Great," 47
Holiness Code, 69-70
Hymns, 27

Immanuel, sign of, 58
Irony, 133
Isaiah, 57-58

Jeremiah, 59-62, 82
Jeroboam II, 43
Jesus, teachings of, 100-101, 104-6, 131; actions of, 102-4, 131-32; death of, 118-20, 136-38; resurrection of, 120-23, 138-39; identity of, 106-8, 134
Jewish-Roman War, 112

Index

Jezebel, 55, 81
Job, 16-21
John (author of Revelation), 77-78
John Mark, 98
John the Baptist, 99-100
Josiah, 43-44, 68-69
Judges, 40-41
Justice, 55, 56-57, 61, 66-69, 72, 79

Kingdom of God, 76-77, 100-101

Laments, 27-29
Law codes, 66-72
Law, oral, 105
Letters, 80-91
Logos, 135-36
Lord's Prayer, the, 31-32
Lord's Supper, the (Eucharist), 32, 86, 114
Luke the evangelist, 127

Maccabean (Hasmonean) revolt, 45-47, 75
Marriage and divorce, 85
Messiah, messianism, 30, 44, 59, 64, 108, 110
Miracle stories, 102-4
Moses, 37-38, 109, 105

Nebuchadnezzar, 44, 75
Nehemiah, 45
"New Testament," 4, 6-8

"Old Testament," 4-6
Omri, 43
Oracles, 54-55

Parables, 100-101, 104-5
Parallelism (in poetry), 145-47

Pastoral letters, 83-84, 90
Paul, 48-51
Paul's letters (Pauline corpus), 7, 83
Pentateuch, 5, 46
Peter, 48-49
Prehistory, 36-37
Prison letters, 90
Prophetic literature, 54-65
Psalms, 26-33

Q (Gospel source), 95

Reading biblical literature, 1-3, 24-25, 32-33, 51-53, 64-65, 71-72, 79, 90-91, 139-40, 141-43
Resurrection of the dead, 86-87
Righteousness, 88, 125
Royal psalms, 29-30

Samuel, 41-42
Saul, 41-42
Second Isaiah, 62-64
Sermon on the Mount, 124, 125
Servant Songs, 63-64
Sexual immorality, 85
Solomon, 11, 42-43
Son of God, 108-9
Son of Man, 109
Stephen, 49
Synoptic Gospels, 93
Synoptic problem, 93-97

Ten Commandments, 66-67
Torah, 4, 67, 105, 125

Wisdom literature, 9-25
Wisdom personified, 16

Zedekiah, 44